CW01507608

We kindly ask that you respect the copyright of this book, 'DO THIS TO MANIFEST EVERYTHING' which encompasses all its content, including text, images, and ideas. Permission to reproduce, distribute, or transmit any portion of this publication in any form must be obtained in advance from the author. Exceptions are made for brief quotations used in critical reviews and certain noncommercial uses as permitted by copyright law.

While we've taken great care to ensure the accuracy and completeness of this work, please understand that the author and publisher cannot guarantee its suitability for every reader's needs. The advice and strategies provided may not apply universally.

We sincerely hope that this book enriches your life, but it's important to note that the author and publisher cannot be held responsible for any loss of profit or other damages, whether direct or incidental, resulting from the use of this material. We encourage you to seek professional advice when necessary.

By accessing and using this book, you agree to abide by these terms and conditions. If you disagree, we kindly ask that you refrain from accessing or using this book. We appreciate your understanding and cooperation

ARCHER STERLING

DO THIS

TO MANIFEST EVERYTHING

Do This To Manifest Everything

Archer Sterling

Published by Archer Sterling, 2024.

While every precaution has been taken in the preparation of this book, the publisher assumes no responsibility for errors or omissions, or for damages resulting from the use of the information contained herein.

DO THIS TO MANIFEST EVERYTHING

First edition. October 29, 2024.

Copyright © 2024 Archer Sterling.

ISBN: 979-8224635283

Written by Archer Sterling.

Table of Contents

Introduction

———

There was a time in my life when I struggled to make sense of why my dreams always seemed just out of reach. I was working hard, trying different approaches, and yet, the abundance I yearned for—financial freedom, the joy of true self-expression, a life untethered by scarcity—continued to elude me. It wasn't until a single revelation turned everything around. That breakthrough moment? Understanding and removing a hidden money block I'd carried for years.

What I discovered then, and what I'm about to share with you, changed my life forever. It wasn't about hustling harder, having better luck, or waiting for the "right opportunity." Instead, it was an internal shift. I'd been limiting myself with the very beliefs I held about money, prosperity, and my own worthiness. Under the guidance of Bob Proctor, I realized that my mind, my energy, and my own thoughts about money were my greatest obstacles. He taught me a powerful truth: "It's my right to be rich." And once I let that statement resonate in my soul, my world began to change.

I know, for some of us, saying "It's my right to be rich" might feel strange. We've been conditioned to think that wealth is reserved for the lucky or that it's somehow less "spiritual." But what if you could reframe that? What if the abundance you seek is actually a part of your spiritual journey? Imagine that your desire to experience financial success is actually a divine calling, an invitation to engage more fully with the richness of life itself.

In these pages, I'll guide you through the mindset shifts, affirmations, and practices that can help you align with the prosperity you were meant for. From a fresh perspective on your relationship with money to practical steps you can implement today, this book will walk you through a transformation that's within reach for anyone willing to believe it's possible.

Together, let's remove those subconscious blocks, awaken a new sense of possibility, and affirm that wealth is not only achievable but is also your birthright. This journey isn't just about changing your bank balance; it's about embracing a life of complete abundance and aligning with the expansive possibilities that have always been within you.

Let's start. It's your right to be rich—and this book will help you believe it.

Detoxifying Your Pineal Gland

———

Steps to Reawaken Your Third Eye

Did you know that deep inside your brain, there's a tiny part called the pineal gland, and it's be attacked? It's called the pineal gland because it looks like a little pine cone. Others refer to it as your "third eye" because they believe it can help us perceive things that aren't visible in the real world. I'll tell you a crazy story about that in a minute and how you can do it too. But living in today's world isn't doing your pineal gland any favors. We're constantly exposed to electromagnetic fields, harmful chemicals, and stress, all of which accelerate the calcification

of your pineal glandand and block your third eye..

There are three things you need to know to protect yourself from the dangers presented by our everyday world:

1. What the pineal gland does and why it gets blocked and calcified.
2. How to protect your energy field and shield your third eye from these modern threats.
3. How to unlock it and what happens once you do.

I'll show you exactly how to do all that, but without spoiling too much, let me just say that when I unlocked mine about 10 years ago, I saw my entire future unfold in my mind with precise accuracy, 10 years before it happened. This will change your life because it gives you the answers you need once you understand how to unlock your third eye.

Now, let's start with number one. What is the pineal gland? You've probably heard of it before—it's a small, pine cone-shaped gland in the middle of your brain. It's a real physical structure. People often dismiss the "third eye" concept, but the pineal gland is responsible for many things, including the release of melatonin, which regulates your sleep cycles. It turns melatonin off in the morning to wake us up. But the pineal gland does much more than that—it helps us connect to our inner thoughts, dreams, spiritual realms, and intuition. It allows us to see beyond the veil of illusion that is our everyday reality. This is why it's often called the "third eye."

That brings us to number two, which is calcification. Calcification actually happens in your pineal gland. Here's a photo right here—you can see it's real, visible on x-rays. It's kind of like the plaque that builds up on your teeth. When your pineal gland gets a buildup of calcification, it limits its electrical function, making it harder to produce melatonin. This can lead to trouble sleeping and may block you from accessing your intuition and deeper spiritual parts of yourself.

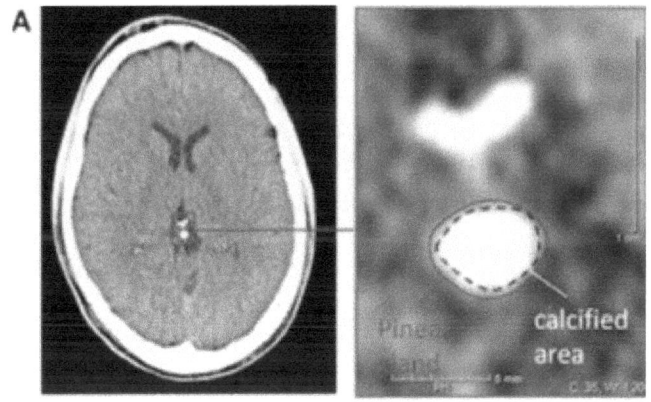

So, what causes this calcification? There are a few main culprits:

Fluoride: This is a mineral often added to tap water and toothpaste. It's a neurotoxin, and there are numerous published medical studies showing that fluoride concentrates in the pineal gland. The pineal gland doesn't have the same type of blood-brain barrier as the rest of the body, so toxins naturally accumulate there. I won't dive too deeply into that now because there's more important stuff to cover, but later I'll show you how to decalcify and unlock your pineal gland.

Unhealthy Foods: Eating lots of processed, unnatural junk food—like sugary snacks and fast food—can make your body more acidic, which in turn helps calcium build up in your pineal gland.

Too Much Screen Time: Spending excessive time on phones, computers, or tablets (something we're all guilty of) exposes your brain to electromagnetic fields (EMFs) and blue light. This disrupts your pineal gland and affects melatonin production. That's why one of the first things people recommend for better sleep is avoiding screens at least one hour before bed—blue light messes with your pineal gland, your circadian rhythms, and melatonin production.

Lack of Sunlight: The pineal gland needs sunlight to function properly, just like all the cells in our body. When we stay indoors all the time and don't get outside, we're not recharging our brain's "batteries." Your entire body is energy, and the pineal gland is a conduit of electrical energy. The ultimate source of this energy is the sun. Just getting a few minutes of sunlight each day can help reactivate those cells in your pineal gland that are slowly calcifying.

Pollution: Breathing in chemicals from polluted air or drinking low-quality municipal water can cause problems not only for your pineal gland but for your entire body.

Now, let's talk about how calcification affects your pineal gland. When your pineal gland gets calcified, there are a few key problems. One of the major signs is trouble sleeping. If your third eye is essentially blocked by environmental toxins and calcification, it's safe to assume there's a strong correlation between that and your inability to sleep, since melatonin production is affected.

You'll also notice reduced creativity and intuition. The third eye is your spiritual eye—it sees beyond the physical realm and is synonymous with creativity and intuition. When it's blocked, you lose those intuitive capabilities, creativity, and spiritual insights.

That's why I believe it's so important to understand what we're going to discuss in this chapter. By following what we talk about here, you can unlock incredible intuitive abilities you didn't know you had—creativity, new ideas, and guidance to accomplish amazing things.

So, can you fix a calcified pineal gland? The good news is, yes, you can. Taking care of your health can actually do the trick. First things first, in my experience, one of the most important things is to drink clean water. Not just filtered water, because "filtered" doesn't always mean much. You can Google your city's water supply, and even if you have a water filter, there are still so many contaminants in city water—it's actually crazy. It's shocking that the people running city water systems aren't held accountable. There are things like arsenic and other harmful substances that people don't realize they're putting into their bodies.

Because the pineal gland doesn't have the same type of blood-brain barrier as the rest of your organs, these toxins can pool in your pineal gland. This brings us to the next point: be mindful of what you're putting into your body and use natural products.

For example, I had long hair for many years, and people often asked why my hair looked so good. That's when I realized that people have no idea what they're putting on their bodies, just like they don't always know what kind of water they're drinking. I always used natural products. If you check most shampoos and conditioners, even at places like Whole Foods, they contain a lot of toxic ingredients mixed with perfume to make them smell good, but they aren't actually good for you.

It's important to pay attention to everything you put on your body—from lotions and face creams to sunscreen. Check for additives and chemicals that may not be good for you, especially in shampoos and conditioners. Many of these products contain harmful substances, and it's essential to be aware of what you're using.

Next, make sure to get plenty of sunlight. Even if it's not direct sunlight the whole time, try to get at least 15 or 20 minutes of exposure every day. It doesn't have to be direct sunlight if you have sun sensitivities—just being outside, even in the shade, is beneficial. Like a sponge absorbs water, the cells in your body absorb natural light, and this is incredibly important.

Another tip is to avoid screens at least 15 minutes before bed. I usually aim for 20 to 30 minutes, but this week I started a new routine where I avoid screens for an hour before bed. What I do now is turn off my phone, go for a walk, and then go to bed. This helps avoid screen influence on my pineal gland, especially before sleep. Not only will this help open your third eye, but it will also help you sleep better.

The Law Of Detachment

Unlock Success By Letting Go

What I'm about to say may not make any sense—it might sound weird, and you may not fully understand it consciously, but I guarantee it will make you rich. In fact, it made the actor Matthew McConaughey 160 million dollars. It's called the law of detachment—basically, not caring about money, not caring about your goals, not caring about what other people think, not caring if you succeed or fail—not giving a crap. That energy actually makes you insanely rich, and I'm going to show you how to do it in three easy steps

that will change your financial life forever.

Step number one: the world reveals itself to the one who needs nothing. That's a quote from the *Tao Te Ching*, an ancient Chinese text from thousands of years ago. It's also one of the key takeaways from McConaughey's book *Greenlights*, which I just finished reading. It's a fascinating book, and I was laughing so hard because when he finally decided he wanted to become a big, famous, rich, successful actor, he moved to Los Angeles. He met a big, successful guy in the industry who invited him to stay at his house until he got on his feet and started making some money.

The first night at dinner, Matthew asked the guy, "Hey, can you help me get an agent and a manager? I really need money. I'm running out, and I need someone to make some phone calls for me and get my foot in the door." The guy was super direct and basically told him, "Shut up. Never say that again. Get out of my house and don't come back until you don't need money or success. This industry will give you everything once you realize you don't need anything from it. As long as you need something, you'll never be successful. But as soon as you realize you don't need anything, they'll all want you, and you'll be huge."

So, the next day, McConaughey leaves and goes on a motorcycle trip through Europe for a couple of months. He doesn't come back until he feels this deep sense of connection to himself and a renewed sense of aliveness. When he returns, he knocks on the guy's door and says, "Hey, I'm ready now." During dinner that night, the guy notices the change and says, "I can feel your vibe is different—clearly, you don't need anything now. Perfect. I've got meetings set up for us tomorrow."

That week, McConaughey lands a management deal with one of the biggest talent agencies, and his career takes off from that point. It's an awesome story because it wasn't until he quit needing the jobs, quit needing to make money from the jobs, and quit needing the end result of being a rich and successful actor, that everything changed. Once he stopped needing it and even stopped thinking about it, he just showed up as himself—like, "Hey, I'm Matthew McConaughey." When he was in that vibe, all the money and job offers started coming in. As soon as you stop needing, that's when the money arrives. But when you need it, it never comes.

That's because neediness is creepy—creepy on a subconscious level. Also, money has ears—it hears when you call. You can even say that to yourself: "Money has ears and hears when you call." What does that mean? It means that on a subconscious level, you're always talking to money. You're either calling money into your life or asking it to leave, depending on whether you're in a place of abundance or a place of need.

It's the same idea as going on a date with someone who's overly clingy. Imagine meeting someone and after just five minutes, they say, "I need to never be alone again. You need to come home with me. Let's handcuff ourselves together because I never want to be apart from you." That would be creepy, right?

That would be beyond creepy—actually repulsive. You'd leave immediately. Needing is creepy. You only get what you want to the degree that you don't need it. When you need something, you're trying to fill a void within yourself, which means you aren't in vibrational harmony with wealth, money, success, your dreams, or your future. When you're not in harmony with it, you crave it because you're trying to fill that space within yourself. But when you realize you don't need it, it starts to come quicker, easier, and faster.

You don't need the money; the money needs you. When you understand that, the money will come. All the things you can buy with money are great—yes, a sports car is fun, and a nice house is cool—but you can be just as happy camping. One of the happiest times in my life was when my wife and I were living out of a Prius in the Northwest, just before we decided to start a family. We spent an entire summer camping, moving from place to place, staying in national forests for weeks at a time. We didn't have much, but we were happy, just sitting by rivers and soaking up the sun.

The craziest part? That's when my business grew the most, and I made the most money I'd ever made, all while I wasn't working. I was simply connected to nature, not caring about anything else. That energy caused things to happen. When you stop needing it, you reinforce that you are already good enough, already worthy. There's nothing you need, and when you're in that energy, all the things you want come to you.

Step number two: We'll talk more about Matthew McConaughey's stories from his book. Step two is: find out who you are, and don't be afraid to be that person, even if it's totally different.

In McConaughey's book, once he started to gain success and build his buzz in Hollywood, he entered a "screw it" phase. He didn't care anymore. He had already found himself during his time riding motorcycles and traveling, so now that he was famous, he was almost repulsed by it. He landed a huge movie gig, and in this "screw it" mindset, he decided to shave his head completely bald, right after signing the deal.

The next day, tabloids were filled with pictures of McConaughey bald. The film director called him, furious, and raised his voice cussing him out, telling him he had ruined the movie. But instead of apologizing, McConaughey doubled down. He decided to walk around everywhere with his shaved head, making sure everyone saw it.

There was a big Hollywood event coming up, and McConaughey went, proudly displaying his bald head. The next day, the same director called him back, but this time with a different attitude, praising the bald look and saying it was going to be the next big thing. What happened was, the director saw McConaughey at the event and noticed how everyone was reacting to him—realizing McConaughey had been right all along.

The lesson McConaughey took from that was this: until you can tell the world or your industry to screw off, you won't be successful. His exact quote was, "Hollywood loves you only when you stop caring about it accepting you."

I think it's the same way with almost anything, and it's the core of the law of detachment. When you care so much about what other people think—if I cared so much about what everybody said in the comments, I could get so obsessed with criticizing myself that I'd never make another book. You can get so caught up in what everyone says about your business, the book you're trying to write, the music you're making, your body, your house, your car, your teeth, your hair, or your clothes, that you end up in a place of insecurity. In that state, you can't attract more money, close sales, create a great product that people want to buy, or align yourself with the frequency of wealth and abundance.

When you stop caring about what everyone thinks, like McConaughey says, it brings a lot of money. I mean, the guy is worth—what?—150 million dollars. Clearly, when you stop caring so much, it changes everything.

Step number 3: is to know what you want, set your standards but let go of the outcome. McConaughey was doing romantic comedies, and he was really big. He was making a ton of money, but it didn't fulfill him anymore. He wanted to do serious roles, but Hollywood had pigeonholed him as a rom-com guy, so he wasn't getting offers for other types of work. He decided to stop accepting romantic comedies, even though he was being offered a lot of money for them. He was basically told it would be the death of his career, that if he declined these roles for long enough, Hollywood would stop calling.

So, he went from making millions of dollars a year to making zero dollars for over two years. At one point, he was offered $12–15 million for a single rom-com. He thought, "I need to take this, this is the most money I've ever been offered for one movie. What am I doing?" But he said no. He went an entire year without a single job offer because Hollywood had stopped calling. He thought his career was over and started wondering what he should do with his life.

Then, after more than two years, he randomly got a call for *Dallas Buyers Club*, which he ended up winning an Oscar for. That led to all kinds of other movies, like *The Wolf of Wall Street*, and more serious roles. He probably made more money after that than he did from his romantic comedies, but there was that two-year period where he made nothing. He declined tens of millions of dollars because he knew what he wanted.

Now, the key is to let go of the outcome. It's about knowing what you want and standing firmly in that. That's why this chapter is set up the way it is, and how I built it the way I did—because you can't even get to step number three until you get to step number one & two. Step two is finding out who you are and not being afraid to be that person, not being afraid of whether or not other people accept you. That's why we start with number one: you don't need it. You don't need them, the money, the success, or the validation. It's all already within you, and when you're in that energy, you'll attract what you need.

These first two steps are so important to get to step number three, which is knowing what you want but letting go of the outcome. When you let go of that outcome, there's a certain freeness to you, where money becomes more like a game. When you're strapped for cash, it doesn't feel like a game—it's almost offensive when a rich person says, "It's just a game." We hear billionaires talk about how making money is just like playing basketball or baseball, and we think, "Yeah, easy for you to say!" It feels offensive because we're in survival mode. It doesn't feel like a game when you're having heart palpitations, your hair is turning gray, and you're dealing with a divorce because of the stress. When you're stuck and unable to have any freedom, it doesn't feel like a game.

That's when we're so obsessed with the outcome, and ironically, the more obsessed we are, the more we limit our financial success. But when we let go, we create space for really awesome things—for miracles. Letting go also reveals what we need to work on within ourselves. When I let go, and when you let go, a certain fear may come up—whether it's the fear of not controlling the outcome or of not being good enough. Whatever it is, that's where you know your work is.

When you let go of the need for the outcome, like McConaughey did, you start to stay in such a heightened vibrational state, raising your energy so high that the outside world eventually catches up. The money comes, the big breaks come, and for me, it was like suddenly getting book deals and going from here to there. It just happens one day.

For that to happen, though, you have to let go of needing it and let go of the outcome, making space for the universe to work its magic. When you do that, that's when the money, the success, and all the awesome things come. And when they do, you realize you can enjoy them, but they're secondary. Because at your core, you remember the truth: you're a spiritual being in a physical body, and you're good enough, smart enough, and you don't need any of these things to feel free.

To be totally honest—and a little embarrassingly—I thought the law of attraction alone was going to make me rich and successful, but it didn't. Then I learned about the law of detachment, and in this part of the chapter, I'll explain exactly how the law of detachment will not only make you rich, but help you get anything you want in life, whether it's in your career, health, relationships, or attracting specific people. The law of detachment is the fastest way to get what you want.

Detachment, especially in our Western world, can sound almost paradoxical. First, though, detachment doesn't mean you don't care. For example, when I was 19, I dropped out of college because I had this dream of becoming a big author. It's not that I didn't want it—I just didn't become so enlightened that I could sit in a Buddhist monastery and renounce all desires. I'm just too programmed by Western culture for that. But I reached a point where I didn't care about the outcome. I knew what I wanted.

With the law of attraction, people get so focused on what they want that it becomes a need, where they're constantly asking, *Has it happened yet?* This puts you in an energy of lack. The law of detachment is kind of the opposite. I wanted to be a big author, I had goals, and I knew what I wanted. But I didn't know whether it would work. I was only 19, dropping out of college, backpacking around the world, writing a book—I had no idea if it was going to work. But I knew what I wanted, knew who I was, and believed in a friendly universe.

Albert Einstein has a quote that says you have two choices: to live in a friendly universe or a hostile one, and that's one of the most important questions you can ask yourself. I believed I lived in a friendly universe. I didn't know if it was going to work out, but it was okay if it didn't because I had found something that gave my life meaning. By default, I was already happy. I didn't need success to validate my life or make it feel worthwhile. That's detachment—when you don't need an outcome to complete your self-story, you actually raise your vibration.

Lao Tzu, in the *Tao Te Ching*, says that *the world reveals itself to the one who needs nothing.* The person who needs nothing ends up getting everything because they are free from limitations, lack, and fear. They're not staking their self-worth on getting or not getting that thing. So, remind yourself that you're already good enough, that the kingdom of heaven is within you, and that you don't need anyone else to feel complete.

Imagine you walk up to a stranger you find attractive, but with a sense of desperation, saying, *I don't want to be alone anymore—will you make sure I'm not alone?* They're going to run away! They may even call the police, depending on how desperate you come across. That kind of energy pushes them away. But if you're already happy and had a great week on your own, you don't need them. You just think they'd complement your life because you like their smile or the way they're painting in the corner of a coffee shop, and you like to paint. They'd add to your life, help your overflowing cup continue to overflow. So, when you approach them with that mindset, there's a shift.

All of a sudden, they're like, *Whoa! Unlike the ten people who approached me before, you don't need anything from me. There's something different about you.* It works the same way in sales meetings, starting a new business, or interviewing for a job—when you don't need it, you actually get it quicker and faster, because the world reveals itself to the one who needs nothing.

But after saying all that, it's worth mentioning that being too detached can actually stem from fear. Some people are so afraid of not getting what they want that they never declare it. They never talk to that person, never start that business, because deep down, they're afraid it won't work out. They might say, *I'm enlightened and don't need anything,* but end up doing nothing. Meanwhile, they may struggle to pay for their kids' school or to achieve other meaningful goals. Detachment isn't about sitting on the couch and doing nothing. We're still creating our most ideal reality; we just recognize that we get it faster when we realize we don't *need* it and that the ultimate reality is within ourselves.

So if you want to get what you want faster, let go. But not in a way that has you sitting around saying, *I don't need anything; I'm too cool for this.* Instead, let go and still go talk to that person, start that business, make that call, move to that new city, do the things that scare you. What you're really saying in this state is, *Here's what I want. I'm worthy of it, and I'm not afraid of not getting it. So, universe, show up—I'm waiting, but I'm not afraid if it doesn't work out.* This shift changes your frequency, helping you overcome subconscious fears, childhood limitations, and self-doubt. The quickest way to let go of those limitations is to claim what you want, pursue it, but not be afraid if it doesn't happen.

This mindset works almost like reverse psychology on the universe. That's why I talk about using *Success Hypnosis.* I have some success hypnosis audiobooks on audible, and about a hundreds of thousands of people from all over the world have used it. Every day, I get stories of how it's helping people reprogram their subconscious minds. You can listen to it for a few minutes and start eliminating those negative beliefs, so you can let go and stop worrying about whether your desire is coming. That way, you can let go of inner doubts, beliefs, and resistance against your highest dreams.

So, take a deep breath, and say to yourself, *What do I want?* Claim what you want. After you claim it, let go and show up for it. This shift in your frequency will magnetize it to you.

Trust In God

———

Build Your Relationship With God

W hat if I could show you how to make any of your prayers come true? And what if I could prove to you that God actually wants to give you what you ask for? God wants to fulfill your prayers—the money, the job, the soulmate, the health miracle. It's all written in the Bible, and these are direct, precise instructions from Jesus himself on how to pray for what you want and receive it every single time.

I'm going to show you exactly how to do this. Once you learn it, you can do it in just a few minutes—that's all it takes. Wishing you a beautiful day, and thanks for being here.

Number one: All doors will be opened. "Ask and ye shall receive, that your joy may be full." Not a quarter full, not half full, not sometimes full and sometimes empty, but *pressed down and running over.* That's because, as Jesus said, "All things that the Father hath are mine." All things of God are yours. Comment that down right here "All things of God are mine." Can you really comment that and feel it with absolute certainty? God, spirit—also known as universal Mind, the holy substance—everything it created is instantly available to you, and it is yours because all things the Father has are yours.

This is the consciousness Jesus was guiding us toward—understanding that God is in everything you desire, like your dream house, for example. The house is secondary; it may be incredible, but God is in every single atom, molecule, piece of construction, glass, and drywall in that home. So the thing you desire, like your dream house or money, is really God. And God works within you because you're made in the image of God. Therefore, you're actually *one* with your desire, because it's all part of the divine flow of the Holy Spirit. You are already good enough for Him. What stops most of us is thinking we're separate from what we desire. We think we're not good enough, or that God doesn't want us to have it—even though Jesus said, "All things the Father hath are mine." Knock, and it will be opened. You're good enough; you're a divine being. Meditate on that. When you truly realize God *wants* these things for you, it opens up a whole new reality.

Number two: Jesus said, "Go and do thou likewise," he meant it. He fed five thousand people with two fish and five loaves of bread, and he said, "Greater things than these shall ye do." So why aren't we manifesting these miracles? Why aren't we attracting divine levels of wealth, success, health, and miracles that elevate our lives to a level of excitement where we see God in everything and feel God in every moment?

It's because we haven't fully put our faith in the universal Mind, in God, in the substance of spirit. Jesus invited us to be "in this world but not of it." Yet, sometimes we get stuck in a worldly consciousness, conforming to its patterns, when Jesus said, "Do not conform to the patterns of this world, but be transformed by the renewing of your mind." Sometimes, it may feel like your prayers won't be answered, like your wishes may not be fulfilled, and I get that. But this is when you stop trying to do it on your own. This is when you invite God into your life and affirm to yourself that you are made in the image of God, that you are worthy, and that God wants to manifest through you. God created you, and God created the thing you desire.

The word *desire* itself means "of the Father." It's actually incredible. Did you know the word *desire* comes from the Latin *de sire*—*de* meaning "of" and *sire* meaning "father"? So, the actual origin of the word *desire* is "of the Father." You are your desire. Yet, for some reason, we've come to believe our desires are bad, wrong, unholy, or not godly. But the word literally means "of God," so your desire is actually God wanting to express something through you. You're made in the image of God, and God is in everything—God created everything. Creation is God experiencing itself through you.

So, God put the desire for whatever it is you want inside of you, and God created the thing you desire as well. God wants it through you, and your desire is worthy. It's amazing when you really think about how profound that is. For me, it was hard to wrap my head around because I realized how much I had been conditioned by limiting beliefs—the very patterns of the world Jesus warned us not to conform to. These limiting beliefs are subconscious, like thinking you're not good enough, not smart enough, too old, too young, too fat, or too skinny.

When I started making friends, I had this crooked tooth, and I thought, "People are going to see this and judge me." And sometimes people did comment on it, saying things like, "Yeah, this manifestation stuff works, but you can't even fix your crooked tooth." That's the pattern of the world—those inherited subconscious beliefs that control our lives instead of the image of God. That's why I began reprogramming my subconscious. As I like to say, "Brainwash yourself before the world brainwashes you." I do this by listening to free sucess hipnosis audio videos on youtube.

Now, number three: I invite you to stop limiting God in your own mind. There's plenty more because God is infinite, right? If God fills all space and all time, there can be no lack of abundance, substance, or spirit. The only thing we need to overcome is our fear of lack or the illusion of lack. The Bible says, "For those that have, more is given; and to those that have not, even what they have is taken away." This means those who have a consciousness of God receive more, while those who don't, who lack the consciousness of abundance, remain stuck in the patterns of this world and experience scarcity.

When you're in the consciousness of spirit and see God in all your desires—when you view your desires as God wanting to manifest through you, recognizing God's infinite nature—miracles begin to unfold. Jesus demonstrated this with every miracle He performed, always thanking God in advance. He had a consciousness of faith, acknowledging the miracle in spirit before it happened, fully trusting God.

Sometimes, when things start going well with this mindset, we may doubt and think, "Will this continue? Am I still good enough?" This is us slipping back into the world's patterns. It's not about us. Every time I have a big breakthrough—like when my book gets translated or I receive an unexpected check—it's not me. The problem comes when we take credit for the good or blame God when things don't go as planned. When we do this, we get stuck in the world's patterns, living out subconscious beliefs instead of the image of God.

That's why success hypnosis is so important. What I invite you to do is practice thanking God for miracles, whether it's for a specific thing or just for the energy of abundance, love, health, or excitement. When you thank God, knowing it's already happening, that's when miracles occur. Faith is believing in what your eyes can't see, living in this world but not of it.

In another world, you already have that job, that home, that financial breakthrough. You already have everything you desire because God wants these things through you. Remember, the word "desire" means "of the Father," so your desires are holy.

Start practicing giving thanks for what you want. What I do is turn on my success hypnosis, and it becomes like a prayer. I base it on the principle that "to those that have, more is given." My goal in prayer is to get into the energy of abundance, thanking God as if I already have it—whether it's a soulmate, a new job, health, or financial miracles.

DO THIS TO MANIFEST EVERYTHING

Spend a few minutes each day communing with God in that energy. Don't beg or plead. Instead, thank God for what you desire, knowing it's already yours. Remember, to those that have, more is given, and to those that don't, even what they have is taken away.

I will show you proof that when you pray like this, you can get whatever you want—even something you think is impossible. It may be something you've prayed for before, something you've worked on or tried to achieve but haven't seen results yet. But I will share irrefutable proof from the craziest story ever, and when you pray like this, you get what you want every single time. I'll also show you exactly how to do it.

Now, first things first—step number one is to really wrap your mind around the fact that prayer works. This is one of the craziest stories ever, and if this works with prayer, you can bet that what we're going to talk about will work too. I'll show you how to do it in just a minute. You can use this for anything: for money, selling your house, getting a new house, getting a job, getting a raise, attracting your soulmate, or even a health miracle.

As all the recent hurricanes in America have been occurring, first of all, if you've been affected, or if someone in your family has been affected, we send our positive love and energy. Let me know in the comments if that's the case. I came across this incredible video that shows the power of prayer—it might be the most amazing proof story I've ever seen. There was a tornado heading straight for a woman's house, and she used prayer, and the tornado literally changed direction. It was such a crazy story that *Natinal News* covered it, and the woman got the whole thing on video. So, I want to show you a little piece of that right now so you can see for yourself that what we're about to go over works. please scan the QR code here to see.

ARCHER STERLING

Pretty cool, right? But the question is, how do we do it? Well, your job in prayer is to set the intention for whatever you want. Set the intention, and then invite God, the universe, or the miracle-working presence into the situation. I always say, "The miracle-working presence is moving to and through me. The miracle-working presence is guiding and directing my life." You can say this too, remember "The miracle-working presence directs me."

So, set a clear intention. Be specific—whether it's around health, love, or even if you need exactly $783.46, just to give an example. Don't be afraid to be specific, because when you do this correctly, it's going to work. Now, your job isn't to figure out *how* it's going to happen or to create it all on your own. Your job is to set the intention, invite God or the universe in, and thank God, the universe, or life—whatever you want to call it.

Set the intention, invite, and thank. Don't go into it saying "please" or begging; instead, you say, "Thank you, as you are performing the miracle." You say, "Thank you, God. Thank you, Spirit. Thank you, Universe for x,y and z." You walk into it with this energy, and now you're in a place of miracles. You're in a place of attraction, speaking the frequency of miracles, and that is how you communicate the prayer properly

Unfortunately, most people are taught the opposite. We go into prayer saying, "Please help me, I'm struggling," listing all the bad things. The problem with this is that we're not communicating the prayer properly. We haven't set an intention, we aren't inviting a higher power or the supernatural in, and we're not thanking it for the materialization of our desire before it has occurred. We're missing all three key components. Once we align with those three elements, we can move forward, and that's where things start to become really important.

The most crucial part of prayer is that many people know what they want, but this is where they actually block their prayers from manifesting in their lives. You need to be in a state of allowing or receiving. These are cute words, right? But what do they really mean? To allow or be in a state of receiving means that you're not trying to control or create the outcome yourself; instead, you're allowing the infinite intelligence of the universe to orchestrate it for you. You have faith that it will happen in the right way. When you stop trying to control it or figure out how it's going to happen, you create the energetic space in your life for miracles to unfold.

It's like there can only be one hand on the steering wheel. But when you're gripping the wheel tightly, trying to control every little thing, you're blocking infinite intelligence from taking over. This is what allowing and receiving is all about.

The key to making your prayer work lies in the law of correspondence. It's one thing to go into prayer, know your intention, invite God in, and thank God. You might do all that perfectly, but if, after the prayer—or even during it—you're still freaked out, you're blocking its effect. Maybe you need money by next week, or something critical has to happen, and you're feeling anxious, like it's already too late. That emotional energy is not in harmony with the energy of your prayer.

Emotion is energy in motion—there's a frequency behind it. If your emotions are out of alignment, they aren't corresponding with the energy of your prayer. This is why, as the Bible says, "To those who have, more is given." When you already feel it, when you're already in the emotional state of having what you desire, you win. But "to those who don't have, even that which they have will be taken away."

So, even if you pray correctly but then feel stressed, unworthy, or stuck in the old problem's energy, you're negating your request. You must be in emotional harmony with the outcome you're praying for, not stuck in the energy of lack or fear.

The Bible says, "Knock, and the door will open." But it's like knocking and then doorbell ditching God. You knock on God's word for your prayer to be answered, but then you run away before God even opens the door because you're not on the right frequency. It's crucial to ask yourself a simple question: "How would it feel if this happened?" This is where gratitude becomes important. When you can practice thanking God, not just by saying "thank you" but by truly feeling it deeply, it can change everything.

Have you ever experienced this with kids? Right now, I'm teaching my four-year-old all about manners. I'm a bit of a stickler because my parents were, and it's one thing when my daughter says "please" or "thank you" just because she knows she has to in order to get what she wants. It doesn't mean much because it's not coming from a sincere place.

For example, we make watermelon juice popsicles, and usually, my daughter will ask for one, and sometimes she'll get a little demanding about wanting another. There was one time in particular when she freaked out because she wanted a second popsicle. I had to tell her, "First of all, we're only having one. Second, you're not even asking nicely, so why should you get another one?" It was a bit of a teaching moment for her about patience and politeness. Fast forward a couple of weeks later, she came to me in a completely different way. She said, "Dad, I know you've already given me a popsicle earlier today, but may I please have one more?" The way she asked was so polite, so sincere, that it absolutely melted my heart! I couldn't help but smile, and I was so happy to give her another one. I immediately jumped up, grabbed her a popsicle, and handed it to her. I even joked, "Here, take 10!" It was one of those moments that showed me the power of asking in the right way—with kindness, respect, and gratitude.

It's the same way with God and the universe. When we ask for something, it's not just about the words we say, but about the energy and sincerity behind them. Just like how I was eager to give my daughter another popsicle because she asked in such a genuine way, the universe responds to us in a similar manner when we're in a state of gratitude and appreciation. That's when things start to unfold in our favor.

When you get into the energy or emotion of being grateful for something, even though it hasn't happened yet, that speeds up the process of it coming into your life. So, my friend, I invite you to give this a try.

Avoid The Black Hole

———

Evaluate Your Relationships

Hey, have you ever been around someone so negative it feels like they're draining all the positive energy out of you? Being around negative people can actually stop us from creating the life we want if we don't know how to protect ourselves from their negative energy. In this

chapter, I'm going to show you how to do just that.

Tip number one: "That's not part of my belief system." First, you need to understand that no one can make you think something you don't want to think. There's a famous story about Viktor Frankl, who survived the horrors of Nazi concentration camps during World War II. He wrote a book called *Man's Search for Meaning*, where he explains that although he was physically imprisoned, no one could control what he chose to think. He had the power to choose his own thoughts, no matter what was happening around him. That was the one thing they couldn't take from him.

When negativity comes at you—whether someone's complaining about their day, telling you your dreams won't work out, or maybe you're doing it to yourself—just say, "That's not part of my belief system." This means you're choosing not to accept their negativity. You get to decide what you believe. Just because someone else is negative doesn't mean you have to believe it. When someone is negative, you can just think, "I understand where you're coming from, but that's not part of my belief system." You have the free will to believe what you choose. The biggest problem isn't that somebody is negative; the biggest problem is that we absorb and accept their negative ideas. For example, if I come up to you and say this or that, you don't have to believe it. You can simply say, "Thanks, but that's not part of my belief system." You don't need to yell or say it in a condescending way—just calmly say, "Thank you, but that's not part of my belief system."

Tip number two: Remember, you are your own energy. No one else can make you feel a certain way unless you allow them to. When someone is negative, whether it's a friend, family member, or coworker, you can choose not to let their negativity bring you down to their emotional level. They can't make you feel any way—only you can do that. The key is to not get sucked into the idea that someone else made you feel a certain way. Creating your reality means controlling your feelings and living in the emotions of your dreams already fulfilled. This is why it's crucial to reprogram your subconscious mind, as it controls 95% of your life. Using success hypnosis, which is free to use, is the best way to do this, you can find manny on youtube.

Tip number three: Don't go as often and don't stay as long. I learned this from Bob Proctor. If being around certain people brings you down, don't visit them as often, and don't stay as long when you do. You don't need to argue or explain yourself—you just need to recognize that some people operate at different frequencies. This doesn't mean you don't care for them or love them; it just means you might need to limit your time with them.

It's important to note that if someone is always negative, at some point it becomes a form of self-sabotage to guilt yourself into being around them more than necessary. Surrounding yourself with people who consistently drain your energy is a form of self-hatred or self-sabotage.

If you're unsure where someone fits on that emotional range, check in with your body after being around them. Do you feel better or worse? Do you feel uplifted or drained? If you consistently feel drained, remember: don't go as often, and don't stay as long.

Number four is to practice forgiveness. Sometimes people say or do hurtful things out of spite or anger because they don't like themselves or their lives. They project that negative energy as a way to distract themselves from their own inner turmoil. This has happened to you, to me, and to all of us. But when they act in ways we don't like, we must remember that forgiveness doesn't mean we are saying what they did is okay; it means we're choosing to let go of the negative energy so it doesn't weigh us down. When you forgive someone, you're actually freeing yourself. Forgiveness is self-liberation; it's like a weight being lifted off your shoulders or your emotional realm.

When someone does something messed up, especially if it's someone you love—a family member, a close friend—and they're acting out of their own personal issues, it's easy to get angry. Even if you control yourself enough not to project it back at them, you might still feel that resentment building up inside. Forgiving them doesn't mean you have to physically tell them because they may not even acknowledge that they've done anything wrong. They might be in such a chaotic state that if you say, "I forgive you," they might respond with, "You don't need to forgive me; you owe me an apology!"

Forgiveness is an inner process, not something you need to vocalize. It's the alchemy of the soul, restoring lightness and possibility to your own spirit and energy. You don't need to meet with the person or even see them again. Forgiving them doesn't mean inviting them back into your life; it just means letting go to the degree that gives you peace and lightness. It's not an intellectual decision—it's a feeling. Ask yourself, "Do I still feel heavy around this? Is it dense and constricting?" If so, you haven't fully forgiven. If you feel lighter, then you're on your way.

Let me give you an example. I had someone I was really close with, and they went through a tough time, started acting erratically, and it made me angry. I kept asking myself, "Why are they like this?" Finally, I realized that they weren't in a place where I could have a productive conversation, and trying to forgive them openly wouldn't help because they wouldn't accept it. So, instead, I tried to understand. I looked at what they were going through—depression, personal struggles—and realized their actions came from a place of deep misery. I sent them love and, in doing so, forgave them on an energetic level. I let go of the emotional burden, and that shift helped me move forward.

I hope that helps!

Speak With Cosmos

———

Communicate With The Universe

DO THIS TO MANIFEST EVERYTHING

The universe is infinite, right? I think pretty much everyone can agree on that. Science tells us that the universe is infinite, that energy is everything, and energy is omnipresent and always expanding for fuller expression, right? That's what science tells us. So, what if you could communicate with the universe directly? What if you knew how to speak the language of the universe so that you could get what you want quicker, faster, and easier? In this chapter, I'm going to show you five ways to talk to the universe correctly so you can transform your life faster than anyone has ever shown you before. If you're reading this chapter right now, the universe is trying to tell you something critical.

Let's dive into how to change your life by talking to the universe.

The first way to talk to the universe is to focus on the universe's phone number. You know how you've got to dial someone's phone number to talk to them? Once you dial their number, you're on the correct frequency to communicate with them, right? So, the universe obviously doesn't have a cell phone number, so how do you dial the correct frequencies to communicate with the universe? We all want to do that if it's going to help us get what we want quicker and faster, right? That's the whole goal. You want to learn how to tell the universe your goals and dreams, what you need help with, so you can get the universe to help you get what you want faster, right?

Instead of dialing the universe's phone number traditionally, you dial it through where your focus of attention goes. Imagine it's 3,000 years in the future and you communicate with everyone telepathically through the power of your mind. Well, the universe is already that far in the future, and that's how you communicate with the universe right now. Think of the universe as a buddy who's just asking, "Hey, what's up? What do you want to talk about? What do you need help with?" But the thing is, the universe doesn't understand our chit-chat. You're not talking through words and sentences like a normal telephone conversation; you're speaking to it telepathically. It vibes with your energy.

Every time you react to something in your life, it's like you're telling the universe with your focus, "Yep, give me more of this." Life is like being in a massive warehouse. Everything you desire is there, but there are no lights on—it's totally dark. But inside this warehouse, you've got your dream car, your dream house, big bags of money, your soulmate, perfect health, healing, the new job, the promotion—it's all in this dark warehouse. Now, imagine you have one single spotlight, a massive floodlight, and wherever you shine that light on these things, that's what you get. When you're talking to the universe, it's the exact same way, but your spotlight is your point of attention.

That's why Jesus said in Matthew 13:12, "To those who have more is given and to those who don't have, even that which they have is taken away." He was talking about the spotlight of attention. When you focus on something, it's like you're predicting your own future. It's like the universe is holding daily elections, and where you put your focus is what you're voting for more of in your life. If you ignore stuff or feel angry or worried that what you want isn't coming, it's like telling the universe, "No, I'm not interested. No, thank you." The universe is tuning into your focus, not your words or the prayers you're saying in English or whatever language you speak—it's through your focus. That's how you say, "Yes, please," or "No, thanks."

The universe wants to give you more of what you want, but it essentially just responds to the nod of your own attention. You've experienced this before: you bump into someone—maybe at a coffee shop or a grocery store—after having just thought about them, and then boom, they show up. Or perhaps you're thinking about someone you haven't spoken to in a long time, and suddenly, they text you. That's the same way you speak to the universe—through that telepathic communication of focus. The universe's language isn't your native tongue; it's through focus. When you understand this, it all becomes a cool game, leading us into the second way to talk to the universe. This involves understanding the language the universe truly speaks. Let's say you're in Los Angeles, New York, or Europe, and you speak English. Now imagine you're suddenly transplanted to Tokyo, Japan, without a phone, money, or knowing anyone. How would you communicate with the people there if you didn't speak their language? You'd have to learn their language, right? The universe is the same. It doesn't speak Spanish, English, French, German, or Chinese. To get your prayers answered by the universe, you have to learn to talk to it in a language it understands.

The universe is omnipresent and infinite, with the power to create worlds, rearrange subatomic particles, and instantly change your life—your bank account, your romantic life, your health, your career. It's sitting there asking, "What do you want? How can I help you?" But it doesn't understand English. The language the universe speaks is the subtle energy and language of frequency and vibration. That's why the famous inventor Nikola Tesla said, "If you want to understand the secrets of the universe, think in terms of energy, frequency, and vibration." The universe tunes in to our vibes, our frequency patterns—not the words we say.

Every emotion we broadcast, whether frustration, love, or fear, is taken as a request for more of the same. Stanford University research found that we have approximately 65,000 thoughts a day, mostly subconscious. Each one of those thoughts has a specific frequency and vibration. Now, let's keep it simple. Imagine you're thinking thoughts like: "I'm going to be broke; it's hard to make money; I'm not smart enough; rich people control the world, and we little people will always be kept down." How does that feel? It feels like crap, right? But what if you changed it? What if you thought things like: "I'm worthy of everything I desire; money comes to me in new and unexpected ways; I'm in tune with the infinite source of wealth; I'm succeeding in everything I do." How does that feel? That feels good! Every thought and belief you have carries a corresponding emotional state that resonates with your thoughts and beliefs. You know whether you're thinking positively or negatively, constructively or destructively, based on how you feel in the moment, because your emotions are simply electrical impulses firing through your nervous system. In other words, your emotions are waves of energy, frequency, and vibration. And what are your thoughts? Every time you think a thought, you fire electrical signals in your brain. Scientists can measure these electrical signals with machines like an FMRI or an EEG which measure the electrical activity of your brain. So, your thoughts and emotions are coded transmissions of energy, frequency, and vibration. Since the universe's native language is vibration, you communicate correctly with the universe by broadcasting specific vibrational frequencies through your energy, which is controlled by your thoughts, emotions, and perceptions in the present moment.

Again, that's why Jesus said, "To those who have, more is given," because when you feel gratitude, prosperity, excitement, and abundance, you are aligned with your desires. Your emotions and energy tell the universe, "Give me more of this—more money, more success, more love, more of the good things I desire."

This is why I always talk about reprogramming your subconscious mind. You're trying hard consciously to do this, but if your old childhood conditioning was negative, you're still communicating what you don't want. The Stanford study found that 95% of our thoughts are unconscious. So, unless you reprogram your subconscious mind, no matter how many self-help books you read, you'll still be stuck. That's why I recomend free success hypnosis, to help you change how you're subconsciously talking to the universe. By listening to it for a few minutes, you'll start telling the universe to give you more success, more money, and more good things, even if you're not consciously working on it.

Number three is to live in the now because the universe does not understand the past or future. To really communicate with the universe, you have to focus on the present moment. The universe is all about what's happening right now. Since energy is never created or destroyed, time doesn't exist to the universe. When we think about the past or the future, we're essentially sending echoes through space, but the present moment is where the universe is truly eavesdropping and listening to you.

When you're dwelling on the past or worrying about the future, the universe doesn't understand that context; it only perceives what you're expressing in the current moment. That's why, in the book of Job, it says, "The thing I feared has come upon me." If you're worrying about the future, like not having enough money, you're actually sending a poverty signal to the universe. You're speaking to the universe in terms of lack, asking for more poverty because the universe only responds to what you're transmitting right now. To the infinite universe, there is no past or future—only the present moment.

It's fascinating when you really grasp this concept. Even when you're thinking about the past or future, you're still communicating with the universe, unknowingly signaling what you want. To effectively connect with the universe, think and speak in the now. If there's something you want in the future or something you don't want to repeat from the past, you need to change your thoughts and feelings right now.

For example, saying, "I will be happy when XYZ happens" sends the signal, "I am not happy now." Instead, you must believe that you already have the joy, freedom, and success you desire. The universe contains an infinite range of potential realities, all waiting for your request, and when you feel like you've already achieved your goal, that's when the universe begins to align things for you.

The fastest way to do this is through gratitude. Can you give thanks for a future that hasn't yet manifested? Can you express gratitude right now for a job you don't even have yet? Can you thank the universe for your soulmate, even though you're still feeling down about your last relationship? Can you give thanks for your business earning ten thousand dollars, even though your current reality doesn't reflect that?

Once you communicate your gratitude for a future possibility, the universe starts bringing it to you. I know it might sound a bit odd, but when I started thanking the universe for viral books, even though I had only 5,000 readers, things changed. I began feeling grateful for having hundreds of thousands of subscribers that didn't yet exist. Then, out of nowhere, books went viral overnight. Old books from months before started getting millions of views, and I went from fewer than 5,000 readers to hundreds of thousands in just a couple of months.

So, the real question is: can you give thanks for a future that hasn't manifested yet?

Number four is to use your internal GPS system, especially when you're feeling lost. When you're driving a car, you plug the destination into the GPS, and it tells you if you're on the right track or not. If you realize you're not on the right track, you adjust and go the other way, right? The same applies to your thoughts and feelings. Sometimes, you want something, but your thoughts and emotions send mixed signals, pulling you in the wrong direction.

At any point, you can stop and ask yourself, "How do I feel right now? Am I generating feelings that are creating what I want?" What are you broadcasting right now? If it's not aligned with your desires, you can reprogram your internal GPS. You can take a U-turn, recalibrate, and head back toward your intended destination. Your intuition, consciousness, and awareness are your internal GPS—they help guide you. For example, if you want financial success but feel broke, poor, and afraid, you're not in alignment.

Take a step back and say, "I'm so grateful I had money for gas today," or "I'm so grateful I came up with the money to fix my tire, even though it broke." It's easy to get upset, but instead, focus on gratitude: "I really want love, but I'm so bummed it hasn't happened yet. My mind tells me there are no good guys or women left, but I won't think like that anymore. I'm so grateful the universe is bringing perfect love and relationships into my life right now." It feels good to be loved, to know you're blessed.

Abraham Hicks calls this the "Isn't it wonderful?" mindset, and Neville Goddard teaches the same concept. When you get off track, like you're trying to get to Seattle but find yourself in Texas, you simply adjust, just like with your GPS. If you want money but feel like you're stuck in poverty, shift back to abundance. Ask yourself, "Isn't it wonderful that XYZ is happening? Isn't it wonderful I had the money for this? Isn't it wonderful there are billions of potential soulmates out there?"

This shift in mindset brings you back to broadcasting your desires effectively to the universe.

Now, the fifth way to communicate with the universe, in my opinion, is the most important: *repetition*. Repetition is what shapes your subconscious mind, which, as we discussed, plays the biggest role in your dialogue with the universe. Since you were a child, your subconscious has been like a giant sponge, absorbing everything it experienced. Especially as a child, your subconscious didn't know the difference between real and imaginary, or between positive and negative beliefs. It was like an empty cup that got filled with many negative programs, which now control your habits and beliefs.

Psychologists tell us that over 70% of the subconscious programming we receive by the time we're 18 is negative and repetitive. A good question to ask is, "What beliefs, habits, emotions, and thoughts did I get programmed with that I don't want?" Ideas about money, success, confidence, love, relationships, and happiness—what were you taught about your own goals?

The great news is that science has proven you can change your subconscious programming through repetition. You're not stuck with what you inherited. Scientists tell us you can rewire the synaptic connections in your brain. Once I learned that, I decided to experiment with it. I started listening to success hypnosis every day, just to see how far I could go. At the time, I was earning under $2,000 a month, and within a few years, I was a millionaire in my 20s. My books were being published internationally, and I met my wife, Ashley. After it all happened, I sometimes scratched my head, thinking, "Damn, it was this easy all along, and I never knew?" I had been fighting against crappy subconscious belief systems.

You can start communicating with the universe the same way, just by spending a few minutes a day listening to success hypnosis. The universe responds quickly—you'll see new job opportunities, relationships, promotions, or unexpected money showing up. One guy even claimed he won a local lottery by listening to success hypnosis every day for a few minutes.

So, I hope you enjoyed this chapter. These are five ways you can communicate with the universe. Remember, you live in a friendly universe, and you're not alone. The universe is always listening; you just have to learn how to speak its language. That's when the magic starts to happen.

If you enjoyed this chapter, please leave a positive review, and I'll see you in the next one.

YOU CAN FIND MY AUDIOBOOKS ON AUDIBLE TO REPROGRAM YOUR SUBCONCIOUS MIND, JUST SEARCH ARCHER STERLING AFFIRMATIONS ON AUDIBLE

The Seven Signs

———

what you want is on the way!

I made this chapter just for you. If you're wondering, "Is my soulmate coming? Is the money coming? Are my goals going to manifest?" you might feel like you're doing all the right things, yet nothing's happening. Now, you're confused or even doubting. Or maybe you're

just questioning whether you're on the right track.

The thing is, there are seven main signs from the universe that what you want is coming. These are the most common signs I've noticed every single time I've had a huge breakthrough—whether it was attracting money, my soulmate (who is now my wife and the mother of my children), or anything else. These seven signs will show you that you're on the right track. If you're not doing them, they're easy adjustments to make that will open the floodgates for what you want to come quicker and faster.

Number one is that you stop complaining about not having what you want. This is the biggest sign that you're about to attract it. When you stop complaining about not having it, you're now in vibrational alignment with having it. The universe operates under the law of attraction and, more importantly, the law of vibration. The law of vibration says everything is energy, and every emotion and state of being has a vibrational frequency.

When you're in the frequency of wanting money or a soulmate, but you're frustrated, thinking, "It's not happening yet, I've been doing everything, and it's still not happening," your vibration is out of alignment with what you want. But when you stop complaining, you immediately shift into alignment with your desires. One of the easiest ways to do this is to remember: what you want *wants you*, and it already exists. The idea that you might not get it is just an illusion created by your mind. Quantum physics shows us that energy is never created or destroyed, so what you want already exists. Once you realize that, there's no reason to complain because you know it's on the way. There's just a gestation and incubation period, and it might be closer than you think. Wallace Wattles said, "Lack of evidence is not evidence of lack." Just because you can't see it doesn't mean it's not coming. It's closer than you think.

Number two is blessing what you want when you see it in others. If you're in a place of wanting something, and when you see someone else with it, you feel angry, frustrated, jealous, or envious, that's a clear sign you're not going to attract what you want. For example, if you want a promotion and then Billy gets it, and you think, "Damn, Billy, I wanted that," you're blocking your own success. The universe might have been about to give you a different job, maybe a better one. You never know—maybe tomorrow you'll meet your future boss at the grocery store, and it turns out to be a job that's closer to home with 20% higher pay.

The simplest way to fix this is to bless what you want. Instead of seeing someone else's success as taking away your abundance, recognize that we live in a world of infinite abundance. Someone else can't take what's destined for you—it's impossible. When you bless what you want, it signals that you're in alignment with it.

It's like when you play the "Punch Buggy" game as a kid, and after seeing one yellow punch buggy, you suddenly see them everywhere. This happens because of a part of your brain called the reticular activating system, which filters out all the bits of information around you. If your brain processed everything at once, you'd go insane. So, your reticular activating system focuses on what you're consciously noticing. It works the same way with your desires: when you see someone with what you want—whether it's a car, a job, or a relationship—take that as a sign it's coming to you too.

DO THIS TO MANIFEST EVERYTHING

For example, if you see two people in love, instead of thinking, "Do they really need to kiss in public?" you could say, "Hey, that's a sign my true love is coming soon." By blessing what you want, you train your subconscious to bring it into your life.

Your subconscious doesn't know the difference between what you want and don't want; it just takes your thoughts as commands. So if you're envious of what others have, your subconscious gets the message that those things are bad, and it will keep them away from you. Blessing what you want opens up the floodgates for it to come into your life.

Number three is that it becomes real in your inner world. The way you do this is by shutting down your five senses. When your five senses are controlling your life, you're in a state of reaction. That term "visionary," like when people say Steve Jobs or Elon Musk is a visionary, actually means living from an inner vision rather than reacting to the outer world as it is.

To become a visionary is to make what's in your mind real. The first step is to know what you want, and the second step is to create such a clear picture and dwell in your imagination so much that you evoke the emotion of having it. It feels real now. I've researched many studies from major universities. One study took three groups of people learning to play the piano. One group actually played a piano sequence, another didn't physically play but imagined it, and the third was the control group that did nothing. The crazy thing is that on FMRI machines studying brain activity, the group that only imagined playing the piano activated the same brain circuits as the group that physically played it.

What does this show? Your imagination is just as real as physically experiencing something. One way to tap into this is to create a dedicated time for visualization. I invite you to close your eyes and build a picture of what you want that's so vivid, it makes you smile.

When that happens, it means you've embedded it into your nervous system, and your brain has created the new circuits. When that occurs, your outer world changes because you move from a reactionary state to a state of creation, and that's when everything shifts quickly in your life.

Number four is that you feel like you don't need it anymore. Lao Tzu, who wrote the Tao Te Ching, said, "To the person who needs nothing, the whole world reveals itself." Once you live from a state of creation, rather than reaction, and create a life that feels good on the inside, regardless of external factors, the external things—the house, car, soulmate—all become icing on the cake. When you don't place all your importance on them, you realize they aren't essential for happiness, and paradoxically, this brings them to you quicker.

In the Bible, it says, "To those who have, more is given. To those who do not have, even what they have will be taken away." What does that mean? When you're in a state of needing or desperation, where your happiness depends on something external, you'll continue to wait forever. The outside world is a holographic mirror of your inner state.

The goal is to be happy regardless of whether you get what you want. I didn't meet my wife until I let go of the need for a girlfriend or soulmate. I reached a point where I realized how silly it was to be moping around, feeling depressed because someone else didn't want me. I'm alive once, stuck in this body—I might as well be happy.

When you apply that mindset to money, goals, houses, cars, relationships, or health, you gain cosmic power. The person who needs everything is easily fooled, falling for traps and scams, and ends up in the wrong situations. But when you don't need it, everything is given to you, and you can enjoy it. When your happiness doesn't depend on external things, in a world of free will, you receive them instantly.

Number 5 is that you've developed a personal relationship with a higher power, and you trust that relationship. You can call it God, Spirit, Universe, or anything—Billy, Frank, Susie. As Alan Watts said, you can't get wet by the word "water." But when you've developed this personal relationship with a higher power, you realize, as the Bible says, "The kingdom of heaven is within." You understand that you are a divine being, and when you realize that God is on your side, your outer reality aligns with the way you perceive it.

Dr. Bruce Lipton, a cell biologist, proved that the perception a person holds influences the cells of their body on a chemical level. If you believe you're alone in this world, you're automatically in a fight-or-flight state, which affects your cells, vibration, and reality. This reinforces the idea of a hostile world. On the flip side, Albert Einstein once said, "The biggest decision you ever make in life is if you live in a friendly or hostile universe."

When you develop a personal relationship with this higher power—God, Spirit, whatever you call it—you can start to communicate with it. For instance, you can ask for a sign, like, "God, prove to me I'm on the right track," and then maybe you get an extra hundred bucks or set up on a blind date with someone special. When you're in this place, you naturally lose doubt because you know a higher power is guiding you. You weren't created to suffer—you were made to experience the fullness of God's abundance. Everything, from first-class flights to beautiful homes, was created for you to enjoy, and if you're connected to this higher power, it wants you to experience those things. To start, just close your eyes and begin communing with this higher power. Talk to it, and soon you'll see this connection reflected in your life.

Number 6 is that you become aware you're a divine being. When you understand that you're not just this physical "meat suit," everything changes. Most people inherit childhood programming that makes them feel something is wrong with them. For example, when I first started making friends, I was self-conscious about my crooked tooth. I thought it would distract people because newscasters always seem to have perfect teeth. I used to micro-analyze why I wasn't good enough and why my relationships sucked. But then I began affirming, "I am a divine being worthy of what I want." Once I embraced this, not only did I love myself more, but my friends becames super supportive. Everything you want is already here, with your name on it, but it can't come to you until you feel worthy of it. The quickest way to get what you want is to realize you're not only worthy but also a divine being. If you're made in the image of God, one with God, and every cell of your body is a part of the Holy Spirit, then you are meant to experience all of God's creation.

Think about how exciting that is—you are meant for greatness. You're not meant to live in an apartment you hate forever. Maybe you're meant to embrace it, learn the lessons, appreciate it, and then that shift will take you to a new financial level. But you're not meant to stay stuck. So, affirm to yourself "I am a divine being, worthy of everything I desire." That's why it's so important to reprogram your subconscious mind.

I highly recommend listening to free success hypnosis videos on YouTube, or even on Audible, Apple Music, or any streaming platform that offers these success hypnosis MP3s. Just listen for five minutes a day, and it will begin to shift your subconscious programming, eliminating those limiting belief systems that make you feel inferior. Soon, you'll realize, "I *am* good enough!"—and that's when everything starts to mirror that. The people you attract will change because they reflect your new level of self-worth. They treat you better. Business relationships improve, and new romances are with someone who treats you well. The financial success you seek will follow naturally as a result of this inner shift.

Number seven, last but not least, is that every day, you're ready to receive unexpected abundance. Being in a state of receptivity is key to quickly bringing more of what you want into your life. Most people live with closed minds, too attached to their five senses and what they see and experience. They can't comprehend that there's more in store for them because they've been neurologically programmed—through their nervous system and brain activity—to evoke negative emotions tied to their circumstances: their empty bank account, the boss they hate, the job that sucks, or the failed relationship. This becomes a kind of negative homeostasis they're afraid to leave because it's familiar, even though they want to, because it sucks, right?

One of the quickest ways to change this is to shift your mind into a state of receptivity by saying, "I'm open to receiving all the good life has to offer today." Repeat it: "I'm open to receiving all the good life has to offer today," and make it a little game. Use the emotion of anticipation to attract something new. Start with something small: see if you can attract an extra $10, $50, a new business opportunity, or a new client in the next 24 hours. Go for it! See if you can attract a new person, a new possibility for a house, or even something minor. Set a clear intention for what you want to attract, and then repeat, "I'm open to receiving unexpected good, open to receiving all the good life has to offer."

What happens next is eye-opening: when those things start to manifest, you realize, "Holy crap, I can actually control my reality!" This opens you up to new possibilities, and your life can reach a level you never thought possible.

These are the seven signs that you're closer than you think—what you want is on the way!

The 21 Day Challange

Try This Manifesting Techniques For 21 Days And See Your Life
Change

DO THIS TO MANIFEST EVERYTHING

I have a question for you: what if you could use an ancient sleep technique to actually trick your mind into manifesting anything you want? Neville Goddard explains a little-known sleep technique to help you do exactly that so you can achieve everything you want in life with very little effort. I admit it sounds too simple and too good to be true, but I've used this method to go from a struggling business owner to building a multi-million dollar company. I've also used it to attract viral books that helped my audience grow from 5,000 to almost 1 million. I've come to the conclusion that you can use this sleep technique for just about anything you truly desire, and it will reprogram your subconscious mind. However, it's crucial that you read this entire chapter, if you perform any of these steps incorrectly, it will not work. So, if you're ready to reprogram your mind while you sleep and turn it into a magnet to attract what you want, get ready for something

awesome!

If you've heard of Neville Goddard, then you've likely heard him discuss the importance of sleep as a manifestation tool. But if you're anything like me, you're probably wondering how he actually discovered this so-called sleep secret. I found some very old audio lectures of Neville discussing his first encounters with the magical power of sleep and how you can use it, so i will tell you this old quote now and let him explain.

"At the time, I wanted to make a trip to the islanders in the Western team, but I had no money. He explained to me that if I would, that night as I sleped into New York City, assume that I was sleeping in my earthly father's house in Barbados, and go to sleep in that state, I would realize my trip. Well, I took him at his word and tried it for one month. Night after night, as I fell asleep, I assumed I was sleeping in my father's home in Barbados. At the end of that month, an invitation from my family came inviting me to spend the winter in Barbados. I sailed for Barbados in the early part of December of that year. From then on, I knew I had found this savior in myself. The old man told me that he would never fail; even after it happened, I didn't believe it would have happened anyway. That's how strange this whole thing is.

Now, Neville ends that clip with the word "strange," and "strange" is a good way to describe the power you hold before sleep. This sums up the big idea number one: sleep is a magical time for manifestation. Do not knock it until you try it! Keep reading, and I'll explain how you can have these same amazing things happen for you with a lot less work than you can possibly imagine.

Now, this probably sounds good, right? Wouldn't you like to be able to use it? But you might feel skeptical, like I was—like, "Huh?" Or maybe you're unclear on how to actually use sleep to reprogram your mind so that you can attract whatever you desire. So, let's have Neville explain the practical technique here in a very old lecture clip that I found.

"You simply know what you want. When you know what you want, you're thinking of that. But that is not enough; you must now begin to think from it. Well, how could I think from it? I am sitting here and I desire to be elsewhere. How could I, while sitting here physically, put myself in imagination at a point in space removed from this room? I make that real to me quite easily. My imagination puts me in touch with that state. I imagine that I am actually where I desire to be. So can I tell that I am there? There's only one way to prove that I am there. for what a man sees when he describes his will; he describes it relative to himself. What the world looks like depends entirely upon where I stand when I make my observation. So if, as I describe my will, it is related to that point in space I imagine that I am occupying, then I must be there. I am not there physically, no, but I am there in my imagination, and my imagination is my real self. When I go in imagination there, I shall go in the flesh also. When in that state, I fall asleep; it is done. I have never seen it fail."

Now that sums up big idea number two: use sleep to dream that you are already there. This is exactly why I created a very advanced audio sleep technology to help me fall asleep faster, sleep better, and actively reprogram my mind while I was sleeping. I started doing this about seven years ago when my business was making under $2000 per month. By the time I was 27 or 28 years old, I became a millionaire, and my life changed forever.

I turned this into a subliminal sleep system that you can turn on before you go to sleep. It helps you fall asleep and plays while you're asleep to reprogram your mind. This is called Sleep Hypnosis: Sleep and Get Rich. If you want to check it out, manny are available on youtube.

Now that we've had Neville explain how this works, it leads us to big idea number three: think from what you want, not of what you want. Here's a very old lecture where Neville explains the importance of this as you're going to bed each night. What I do is turn on the Sleep and Get Rich system, put myself in that state of mind, allow the subliminals to play, and then I focus on what I want.

Here's the clip of Neville: "Here is a practical technique. The first thing you do is know exactly what you want in this world. Once you know exactly what you want, make as lifelike a representation as possible of what you would see, touch, and do. For example, suppose I want a home but have no money. I would still make as lifelike a representation of the home as I would like. Without taking anything into consideration, I would imagine that home with all the details I desire. Then, at night, as I go to bed, in a drowsy, sleepy state—the state that borders upon sleep—I would imagine I am actually in that house. I would imagine stepping off the bed onto the floor of that house, walking through the rooms, touching the furniture, feeling it as solid and real. Then, I would fall asleep in that state. I know that, in a way I could not consciously devise, I would realize my house."

I absolutely love that! The reason this is so important is that when you're going to sleep—or even when you're just visualizing during the day—you're conditioned to believe in linear time. So, you think about what you want as if it's in the future. You think, "Man, I'd really like that house, I'd really like that car, I'd really like to double my business, I'd really like to attract my soulmate, I'd really like to heal my health." This puts you in a state of "I do not have." And in the Bible, it says, "To those who have, more is given; to those who don't have, even what they have is taken away." So, when you go into it not having, you're essentially putting your subconscious mind in a state of lack. When you fall asleep, your brainwave states slow down, and your conscious mind shuts off. Whatever state of consciousness you're in goes directly into the subconscious, just like updating software on a computer. Whatever goes into the subconscious installs. That's why you have to think from it. When I go to sleep, I'm already in the house, the car, the health I want. It's already there, and then I allow the subliminal sleep system to play. Each time it plays, I enter different dreams, almost like lucid dreaming. People often lucid dream by imagining they're flying or doing something fantastical, but I imagine I'm living in my future already.

What I invite you to do is test this idea. Do a thought experiment for the next 21 days and see what you can attract. Focus on one specific thing: it could be attracting an extra thousand dollars, doubling your business, attracting your soulmate, finding a new friend, or solving a problem. Pick a singular intention. Once you've chosen your intention, let the Sleep and Get Rich subliminal audio system play as you're going to sleep, practice this technique, and allow it to play while you sleep. Do this every day for 21 days. Here's the thing: you have nothing to lose. That's what's so cool about this! It doesn't require extra time or effort; you're already going to sleep. Most people go to bed worrying about their lives, and they are essentially installing that negative operating system into their minds during the most important time: sleep. So, do this 21-day experiment with the Sleep Hypnosis and a singular intention, and then come back and share your success story.

What will happen is you'll start to see evidence. You might wake up one morning and think, "Oh my gosh, I just got a new client," or "Oh my gosh, I just met someone who knows the person who can solve my problem." You'll start seeing it happening all around you because whatever you impress upon the mind before sleep will express itself in your waking hours.

So, my friend, are you ready to see how powerful your mind is? If you are, give this a try! If you love this book, if you enjoyed it, make sure to post a 5 star review. Be sure to check out Sleep hipnosis, sleep system to reprogram your mind for exactly what you want. Thanks for watching reading this chapter, and put a smile on your face because you are more powerful than you believe!

Eradicate Your Old Programing

———

You Need To Reprogram Your Mind

N ow, you may not even realize it, but your life has been shaped by frequencies, and we really don't notice it. If you think about music and how it affects you, sometimes it makes you happy, sometimes it makes you sad, or it energizes or calms you. Music works because it's made up of frequencies, and those frequencies influence your brain and body in ways you can't detect. But it goes much deeper than that—it's not just music. There are countless other frequencies that control how you think, feel, and act. They're shaping and controlling your finances, how much money you make, your health, your relationships, and even

your marriage.

These frequencies are hidden, yet they determine things like whether you're in debt or thriving, whether you attract your soulmate or struggle to find love your entire life. So, I want to show you how you've actually been programmed by these hidden frequencies, and more importantly, how you can reprogram yourself and take control of your life and future.

First things first, the programming isn't visible—we don't really see it. That's because you're not who you think you are. It's like the movie *The Matrix*; it's not science fiction, it's more like a real-life biography about how our lives are shaped from birth by unseen forces. In reality, it's frequencies. Imagine your brain like an iPhone or a computer—it stores everything you know, while you only see the small display of your consciousness projected onto the screen. There's so much happening unconsciously. From the moment we're born, we start absorbing beliefs and ideas, mostly from our parents and the adults around us, whoever raised us. They pass down what they were taught from their parents, and this cycle continues. By the time we're seven years old, 95% of our life is made up of subconscious ingrained behaviors, patterns, and beliefs we've learned from our environment, which shapes our entire perception of the world.

Even as a baby, you start absorbing information in the womb. They've done studies on this. By the time you're four years old, you're in school, following rules, listening for the bell to ring, and being told what's right and wrong, when to speak, and what to believe. These rules begin to shape your entire reality—all these little frequencies we don't even know exist. During those early years, your brain operates in a low-brainwave state called theta. The electromagnetic waves of your brain are in this lower state, which is tied to imagination and learning. That's why kids can take something like a rock and pretend it's a fairy—my daughter is really into fairies right now.

But theta is more than just imagination; it's essentially a hypnotic state. During this time, your mind is like a sponge, or an empty cup, absorbing everything up until you're around 7, 8, 9, or 10 years old. One of the ways this works is through repetition. Since we're babies, we're exposed to the same messages over and over again. These could be beliefs about money, confidence, feelings of insecurity, or lack of self-worth. In this hypnotic state during our early years, we absorb everything and install those frequencies into our subconscious.

And then that controls your perception—how you see the world—which influences what you believe as an adult, what you accept, what you challenge, and ultimately what you create in your life. These hidden frequencies from your younger years shape your adult life. People often wonder, "Why can't I break through financially? Why can't I attract my soulmate?" It's because of those early frequencies. Once you can control your perception, you can break free.

By the time we reach adulthood, 95% of our lives are governed by subconscious programs. Only about 5% of our lives, according to neuroscientists and psychologists, are conscious. That's why people say,

"Give me a child until they are seven, and I'll show you the adult," because that early stage sets the trajectory for your entire life. The amazing thing is that once you understand this, you also have the key to change your future.

Number two is the power of these frequencies. Now that we've kind of established that we've been programmed by frequencies our entire life without even knowing, think about how the news makes you feel—it makes you stressed, anxious, or angry. The words, images, and stories on the news carry specific frequencies, and those frequencies affect you instantly. Similarly, music works the same way, but hopefully, it influences you more positively because music is made up of frequencies as well, and those affect your brain, body, and nervous system.

Everything in life is made up of frequencies. The important thing to understand is that these frequencies ultimately control the state of vibration in your body, or more specifically, your nervous system. Your brain processes these frequencies as electrical signals. For example, when you hear music, your brain decodes those frequencies, just as it decodes other invisible signals in the air around you. The same thing happens with other stimuli besides music.

This is where it gets kind of insidious, because negative energy can control your life without you even realizing it. The crazy part is that you can actually target frequencies into other people's brains to control them negatively. It's a bit dark, so we won't go too deep into that, but there are studies showing that frequencies can be used to make people sleep or perform certain behaviors without them even realizing they're doing it.

At the end of the day, the world around us and the environment we're in aren't always programming us positively; they're not always there to help. Once you realize that, you can start to brainwash yourself before the world brainwashes you.

Now that brings us to number three: really dissecting and becoming aware of the negative frequencies around us. Using the music example again, when you listen to music, you're tuning into certain frequencies, right? Just like a radio, if you're too far from a specific station in your car, the sound starts to get distorted. The same thing happens with frequencies that ultimately control the electrical signals in your brain and the energy programmed into your subconscious mind. This, in turn, controls what you attract into your life.

Schools, the news, social media, parents, movies—all of these install frequencies that shape our entire existence. The problem is that much of this is like listening to distorted frequencies for so long that we don't even realize what pure, harmonious frequency would sound like, Metaphorically speaking, there are harmonious frequencies you can program your subconscious mind with to bring money, love, and your desires into your life, instead of living according to the frequencies that were accidentally programmed into you—either by well-meaning people projecting their own issues onto you or by institutions, corporations, and other sketchy actors attempting to manipulate humanity. by embedding less-than-ideal frequencies into music, movies, social media, and television, these influences affect how society thinks and feels without people realizing it. For instance, they can make people feel anxious or angry for no apparent reason. Then all it takes is a triggering event—like a news story or a public incident—to set off a bunch of built-up emotions that were programmed into people through these frequencies, leading to unrest or other negative outcomes.

I don't want to be the bearer of bad news, but it's important to understand the layers of negative energy that can get poured into your "cup." Imagine your brain as a cup that was totally empty, but without a lid on it, all sorts of things got inside. It's like having a guitar that's out of tune—you're not in tune with your desires, money, love, or health because you, like a guitar, are a vibrational instrument, but you've been out of tune. Most importantly, I'm going to show you how you can actually retune yourself.

To really grasp how this all works, you have specific frequencies, and then you have subliminal messaging. Advertisers have known this forever, too. We're up against years of subliminal programming. For example, studies have shown that if you play French music softly in a grocery store, more people will buy wine. That's frequency programming. And then, when you think about things like MK Ultra, it was all about controlling people's minds and getting them to do things they didn't even know they were doing because their brains were hijacked by powerful frequencies, and they were completely unconscious of it.

Putting aside the darker stuff, if you just look at everyday life, 9 out of 10 people die with less than $10,000. Seventy-five percent of people live paycheck to paycheck. Most people never make significant money or retire in a reasonable time. Over 50% of people are divorced. Financially, the majority of people's energy is programmed negatively. Then, looking at marriages—over half end in divorce—so many people's frequencies around love are also negative. Add to that the racket of the healthcare industry, with so many people living their lives with multiple health conditions. The average person's frequency around health is also programmed negatively.

If you go through any of your desires—whether it's more money, success, love, confidence, or health—the majority of society doesn't have what they want. Most of society is influenced or programmed by negative frequencies.

Especially in your younger years, when you're in a theta brain wave state, you were unconsciously influenced in some respect. In addition to that, a lot of people didn't have good parents or positive influences.

Maybe you dealt with really bad programming, abuse, or things that nobody should have to experience, but you did. You've made it to this moment, though, and now you can free yourself from it because you've become aware. Just like a guitar, you can retune your frequency.

Once you understand all of that—now, once I understood all of this, I was a college dropout, but I wanted to become an author. Bob Proctor always said, "What do you really want? Not what you think you can get, but what do you really want?" What I really wanted was to be a millionaire author and achieve great things. But as a college dropout, I didn't think I was good enough or smart enough. All of that was frequency—at an emotional level—that had programmed me to feel like I couldn't make my dreams a reality. I felt like I wasn't good enough.

So, my frequency programming was down here, but my desire frequency was way up here, and there was no match—no congruence. What I needed to do was reprogram my subconscious mind. Your subconscious controls 95% of your life, and it's your emotional mind, your frequency mind. That's where all the emotions, programs, and frequencies are stored, and that sets up the vibratory rate of your energy field. That field controls your perception, behavior, emotions, and ultimately every result in your life—down to what's in your bank account, how much money you make, and what your relationships and dating life are like.

So, what I started doing was specifically putting new programming into my brain and my subconscious. I created a success hypnosis for myself and started programming my mind, telling myself all day long that I'm a millionaire author, that I'm all these things I aspired to be. Slowly, I started to feel those things, even though they weren't happening yet. I'd get excited while listening to it, brainwashing myself—pouring new things into my "cup." Your cup can be filled with anything—it could be full of gasoline, or it could be full of pristine spring water.

The first step is awareness. You become aware of the unconscious, which is what we've been talking about so far. Then, you pour out all the junk from the cup, and you refill it. Refilling it means putting in the energy and frequency of the emotions that match your conscious desires into your subconscious mind, erasing what you've been taught so you can break free from that old programming. You'll then control your own energy field, which controls your subconscious, ultimately turning you into a magnet for what you want instead of what you don't want.

Now, what I invite you to do is spend two to five minutes a day—it doesn't need to be a long time—putting a new frequency into your subconscious. When you start doing this, there are a couple of important things to keep in mind. First, you want to reject any programming that doesn't align with your new desire. Now that you have this newfound awareness, when negative energy comes your way—whether it's something you saw on social media, someone complaining, or something in the news—consciously reject it.

If you don't consciously reject it, it's like leaving the top off your cup, allowing that energy to enter you. What I like to say in response is, "Thank you, but that's no longer part of my belief system." Make it a mantra, repeating it to yourself until it becomes second nature. This helps build a new mental model to replace the one programmed into you during your early years.

You can say this as a reminder, like a mantra, whenever you encounter negative energy. If someone in your immediate environment brings negativity, you can say it respectfully: "Thank you, but that's no longer part of my belief system." After this, I invite you to "dial in" your new frequency every single morning. Think of it like turning the radio knob to the station you want. You need to set your frequency to the right station before you can enjoy the music you want to hear.

What I suggest is, before you check your phone, the news, or talk to anyone, take a moment to set your frequency. Even if you only have a few minutes—maybe you have kids or a busy life—I encourage you to make a list of things you're grateful for that haven't happened yet. This is where your desires come into play.

For example, if your number one desire is to attract your soulmate, or maybe it's health, a new job, or money, write about it in the present tense. You might say, "I'm so grateful I just got back from an amazing dinner with my soulmate," even if you haven't met them yet. You are stepping into your imagination, tuning into the frequency of your desire. Your soulmate already exists, but you need to embody that frequency first, tuning your "guitar" to that specific note, so to speak.

It might feel weird or silly at first to write about a dinner with someone you haven't met, but remind yourself that's the old program, and say, "Thank you, but that's no longer part of my belief system." Now, I want you to write about what you're grateful for with respect to your desire.

If it's health, write about how you just finished a great workout, even if you haven't done it yet. Or maybe write about how you just hit a new record running the mile. The same goes for money—write about how you just closed a new sale if you're a real estate agent, or how you just received an unexpected thousand dollars. Write about how you got a new job, new clients, or how your YouTube video just went viral. Maybe you sold extra tickets to your event or concert—whatever it is, write it in the present tense as if it's already happened.

By being grateful for these things in advance, you are practicing the emotion of your desire. Essentially, you're tuning your brain, your "musical instrument," to a new frequency—one that matches your desire manifested Biggest reprograms are subconscious, and it starts to shift

I hope you have a great day and that you enjoyed this chapter. If you did, read it again. This information is important. For many of us, myself included, it was new information. I had never heard anything like this before, so it was crucial for me to listen multiple times—not just to grasp it intellectually, but to internalize it as truth. This helps install the new frequency faster, which will shift things like your bank account, love life, health, or whatever you desire.

Wishing you a beautiful day!

Did You Hear That

———

When The Universe Talks, You Listen

DO THIS TO MANIFEST EVERYTHING

Have you ever had a weird ringing in your ears, and you don't understand it? You don't really know if it means anything—like that ringing noise, you know? So where does it come from? I was pretty surprised to learn that the noise actually has an ancient meaning that goes all the way back to the Middle Ages, Ancient Rome, and Ancient Greece. There's actually a spiritual significance to it—the universe may

be trying to tell you something. But what is it?

First, since this seems pretty mundane, and you're probably thinking, "How could that noise have any significance?", let's start by looking at the surprising spiritual meanings throughout history.

The first is the historical evidence of a deeper meaning that goes back to Ancient Rome. In Rome, inspiration was thought to mean that gods, angels, or other dimensional consciousness were speaking to you or whispering to your subconscious. Creative ideas weren't believed to come from your own mind or personality but from a higher intelligence, from another dimension.

Now, if you go back 2,000 years to the ancient Roman encyclopedia of medicine, it gets pretty interesting. The Roman philosopher Pliny's *Natural History* encyclopedia, written over 2,000 years ago, and he was one of the first people to state that ears ringing meant someone was talking about you. So, according to Ancient Rome, the ringing noise you hear is actually a frequency from an unseen world, speaking to you subconsciously.

And that's not the only evidence. In the Middle Ages, people believed that ear ringing was angels talking to you. Many Eastern religions also believe the ringing could be the sound of your chakras or the vibration of your energy body, sound waves briefly occurring at a frequency that you can actually perceive with your five senses.

In Hindu and Buddhist cultures, left ear ringing is meant to symbolize a spiritual awakening of sorts. It's typically associated with your inner voice or intuition, maybe telling you to go in a different direction in life. Meanwhile, in ancient Chinese culture, right ear ringing was seen as a sign of good fortune. But if both your ears are ringing at the same time at different frequencies, that just means you might be going a little crazy! :)

One thing we do know for sure: ear ringing is not a new phenomenon. It's sparked debates for thousands of years. Even Leonardo da Vinci and Charles Darwin experienced it. So, if they experienced it, and you are too, maybe it means you're a genius—just like them!... Im joking, of course.

Now, let's dive a little deeper into what this might really mean and what your subconscious is trying to tell you. Normal hearing involves sound waves interacting with your ear, creating vibrations that are transformed into biochemical and electrical signals. These signals spark cells of recognition in your brain, and in your neural networks, so you are able to instantly recognize what a sound means.

The first memory I have of vibrational frequencies catching my attention was probably when I was about seven years old, and my mom brought home a dog whistle. I had never seen one before, and I was confused. My mom blew the whistle, and our dog came running, but I couldn't even hear it. I remember asking my mom, "How do you know it works?" She replied, "Well, the dog came, didn't it?" But I kept thinking, "Yeah, but what if the dog just came on its own? How come we can't hear it?"

That was the first time I had a brief moment of awareness about the huge, infinite spectrum of different frequencies that exist, and how the physical world might not even be what I thought it was. And that's where it starts to get interesting because if the physical world is just energy, then that means you are more than just your physical body. You are not what you see in the mirror—a spiritual being in a physical body. Your body is like a vehicle or a rental car that you're using for this lifetime. So, when you hear ringing in your ears, what if your subconscious or the universe is tuning your electromagnetic field, similar to how you would tune a guitar? When you use a guitar tuner, each string's frequency eventually aligns. What if that's what's happening when our ears ring? Or maybe it's pointing to something larger, like a reminder that you're a spiritual being in a physical body, and not to get lost in the rat race or the physical world, because you're more than just a body. This whole material world is kind of an illusion, and nothing in it is really as significant as we might think. Maybe the universe is gently pushing you to remember yourself as an energetic, vibrational being.

It's not crazy to consider. Nikola Tesla once said that the secrets of the universe are hidden in energy, frequency, and vibration. He said, "If you want to understand the universe, think in terms of energy, frequency, and vibration." So, when you hear that ringing, what if it's the universe's way of reminding you that there's something more? If back in Ancient Rome they believed that ideas came from another dimension, like angels or higher beings speaking to you, then what if your ear ringing is like Nikola Tesla talking to you right now?

The point is, everything is energy. Sometimes, you might hear ringing in your ears when you're deep in thought, maybe lying in bed, worrying about something, and suddenly your ears ring. You might think, "Oh no, there's something wrong with me, do I need to go to the ER?" depending on how stressed you are right? That's an example of being trapped in the rat race and the physical world, where we become so identified with our thoughts and senses.

But what if the ringing is your subconscious mind throwing you a lifeline, pulling you out of that mental loop of lower-dimensional, lower-frequency thought? It's reminding you: "I am a spiritual being in a physical body." That realization can open you up to see your problems as just energy, not immovable obstacles. What if this is a sign, a synchronicity, inviting this energy into your life to guide and direct you, instead of trying to do everything on your own?

And if you don't try to do everything on your own and instead call this energy into your life, since everything in the physical universe is just energy, then that energy—because there's only one originating substance—can reshape and move your life. That's the universal subconscious mind. We have a subjective version of the subconscious mind, but there's also a universal unconscious mind, which truly connects us to the mind of God. What if the ringing in your ears is like tuning a guitar, but instead, it's the universal mind of God tuning the bandwidth of your electromagnetic field, the mental plane, and your mind's frequency patterns to bring them into harmony? If that were possible, if that were really happening, it would be a pretty significant moment.

I'd love to hear what you think about this. Leave a comment on the review page and let me know your thoughts on these theories and ideas and if you enjoyed this chapter

Write It All Out

————

Manifesti Your Goals On Goal Cards

Okay, I've got a challenge for you. All you have to do is say this Bob Proctor money affirmation, and you will become a millionaire. But here's the kicker—there are three things you need to know about this money affirmation to make it work quicker and faster.

I'm going to share all of that with you in this chapter.

In 2015, the neuroscience department at UCLA University did a fascinating study. They took a group of people, used MRI machines to monitor their brains, and had them practice self-affirmations. Another group did absolutely nothing. What they found was pretty crazy: the neural pathways increased, strengthened, and grew in the group that practiced self-affirmations, while the group that didn't had no results. If you want to get technical, it was the ventromedial prefrontal cortex in the brain that activated when people did self-affirmations.

Big idea number one that I learned from Bob Proctor—rest in peace to his beautiful soul, I know he's out there happy and smiling as we read and create this book right now—is constant spaced repetition. So, what did that UCLA study show? It showed that people using repetition with their affirmations saw measurable changes in their brains through MRI scans—evolutions, if you will. What does that tell you? You can't get the money you want with this affirmation unless you use repetition.

I know this from direct experience because when I was 20 years old, I was super broke, and I met Bob Proctor. He asked, "Why are you so broke?" I said, "I don't know, can you help?" He gave me this affirmation, and I wasn't sure if it would work. I started doing some crazy stuff—listening to it all day long. God bless my wife's soul for hearing it 10,000 times. I'd fall asleep with it, take showers with it, eat with it, stretch with it, play it all day long, say it all day long, write it on paper, and even put it on the treadmill while I ran.

What was I doing, besides being a little crazy? I was using repetition. UCLA's neuroscientific research proves that affirmations, when repeated, create measurable changes in the brain and increase neural pathways. Here's the thing: your current neural pathways are programmed for you to be broke. When you use constant spaced repetition with the affirmation I'm about to share, you'll start making a lot more money.

Big idea number two has to do with this drawing right here—beautiful drawing, if I do say so myself. No, I didn't even draw it; it was created by Dr. Thurman Fleet all the way back in 1932 and popularized by Bob Proctor. Now, to make this affirmation work for you and start bringing more money into your life, you need to find the deep-seated beliefs that are contrary to the affirmation I'm about to give you.

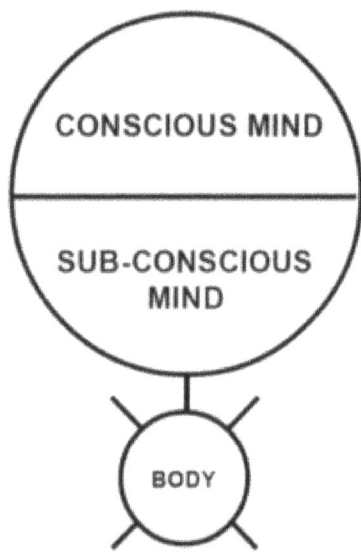

The biggest mistake you can make is jumping into the affirmation without first identifying the deeper beliefs that contradict it. What we have here is a rendering of the mind. When you ask someone, "What is the mind?" they often point to the brain, but the brain is not the mind. The brain is just an electronic switching station. The mind is activity, that's what the mind is. We don't have a clear concept of what the mind looks like, so this drawing is just a visual representation.

Now, 95% of your life is controlled by your subconscious, as Bob Proctor taught, and your conscious mind represents only 5%. So, when you start using this affirmation, it's going to be a conscious action, but you're battling the subconscious mind that controls 95% of your life. When I was on the phone with Bob Proctor for one of the first times, he said, "You know what your problem is? You think you're too young." And I said, "Yeah, well, I am." He responded, "There are 11-year-olds making millions of dollars," and that's when I realized that my belief system was blocking my success.

Another way to look at this is that the conscious mind represents your thoughts, but the subconscious is your emotional mind, the feeling mind. This emotional mind controls your body, which in turn controls your actions and your results. I believed I was too young. I dropped out of college and backpacked around the world. When I wrote my first book, all the publishing companies rejected me, saying I was too young, and I believed them. What feeling did that create? A feeling of inadequacy—that I wasn't good enough. This feeling guided everything I did, and no amount of affirming a word was going to change that deeper emotion.

First, you have to identify that feeling. So, my question to you is: What is that deeper belief you might have that says you can't make more money? Is it that you were told you were dyslexic? That you can't focus? That you might have ADD? That you didn't come from a wealthy family, don't have the resources, or didn't go to the right school? Maybe you think you're too young? First, identify this belief, then you can free yourself from it.

That's why I'm so big on success hypnosis. You can check out a free success hypnosis on youtube. I started doing this after my first year of being mentored by Bob Proctor, and it changed my life. It's free.

The third and final big idea is crazy, but it's going to help this affirmation work a lot better, quicker, and faster to bring money into your life. Big idea number three is: Don't just do the affirmation—become the affirmation.

Researchers at the National Weight Control Registry did a study involving more than 6,000 people who had lost more than 30 pounds, examining the habits of successful dieters. They found that 78% of them ate breakfast every day, a meal cued by the time of day, but they also envisioned a specific reward for sticking with their diet—like a "bikini body," the pride of stepping on the scale, or people telling them they looked great. They focused on craving that reward when temptations arose and cultivated that craving into a mild obsession. In other words, they built a worthy ideal and became that ideal. Weight loss wasn't just an idle goal; it wasn't just an idea in their heads—they literally became it.

While sitting there, imagining having another ice cream or something else tempting, they visualized their perfect body. They imagined how healthy and happy they felt. They became it because the brain is a reward-seeking mechanism that works in pictures. When you give your brain a picture of a reward, you get instant results.

Now, how do we take advantage of this fascinating study? The people who were losing weight effectively had very clear pictures that helped them overcome their old selves. Bob Proctor taught me to use an index card. You just take a little 3x5 piece of paper—Bob calls them "goal cards"—and write what you want in the present tense.

When I was 20, I wrote on my card: "I'm so happy and grateful that I'm a world-renowned author and thought leader, making millions of dollars and inspiring millions of people." I carried this index card with me everywhere. Think back to that UCLA study, and how the MRI showed that repetition of affirmations built new neural circuits and connections in the brain. The index card is always in your hand, in your pocket, or taped to your mirror, constantly reinforcing those pathways.

Most people get excited about making more money, but their old self creeps back in. That's why it's so important, just like in the weight loss study, to have a clear reward in your mind. The index card helps you build that picture and hold it in your mind all the time. I was 21, walking around Encinitas, California, with my sweaty index card in 85-degree weather, and I was seeing a clear picture of myself as a successful author, a millionaire, inspiring millions of people. I didn't know how it would happen, but the picture had already become real to me.

So, pull out an index card. Here are two options of Bob Proctor's affirmations:

1. "I'm so happy and grateful now that money comes to me in increasing quantities through multiple sources on a continuous basis." You can comment this one as a review—"Money comes to me in increasing quantities through multiple sources on a continuous basis."

1. Or, if you want a specific one, write exactly what you want, starting with "I'm so happy and grateful." For example:

• "I'm so happy and grateful now that I'm a world-renowned, successful author and thought leader, making millions of dollars and inspiring millions of people."

• Or: "I'm so happy and grateful that I'm a top real estate agent in San Diego, California, making $120,000 a year."

•Or: "I'm so happy and grateful that I have a fully booked car cleaning

business, making $5,000 a month."

Yours could be anything, but it needs to be clear and summarized in one sentence so that, if a stranger picked up your index card, they'd know exactly what you wanted. It also has to be something you want enough that you'll build the mental picture of it, taking full advantage of all these scientific studies from UCLA and weight loss.

Alright, here's the truth: Most people will never do this. They're going to watch this video, and they won't take action. They won't pick an affirmation, they won't write it down, and they'll continue to be broke. Then, they'll comment on this video, saying, "You don't understand how hard it is."

What are they doing? Think back to the UCLA study. They are further ingraining those neural pathways of being broke, angry, upset, mad at money, and frustrated that their life can't change. But you create your own reality. As UCLA showed us, you're building those neural pathways of being broke, over and over.

Most people won't do it—but I know you will. So, I encourage you to pull out a pen and pad and write your money affirmation down.

So, I encourage you to pull out a pen and pad, write your money affirmation down, and let me know in the comments what you think of this video. Be sure to check out my free success hypnosis, right there down below at Jake's hypnosis.com. Click the button on this video, and I'll see you in the next one.

14 Affirmations For 14 Days

———

Write this each day for 14 days and reap the benefits

O kay, my friend, you see this $20 bill here—it's just energy. Now, take one of your fingers and press it to your thumb, just for a second. Or, move your finger between your other fingers. If you press hard enough, you can feel a little sensation, right? That's your nervous system at work, creating that feeling. But what is that feeling? It's just

an electrical signal—that's all it is.

Now, think about this for a moment—everything, and I mean *everything*, in the entire universe is just energy. That includes your words and even your consciousness. In other words, your *intention*. Your intention isn't just a thought; it's actually a physical force out there in the universe. It's an *energetic* force. And once you really get that, once you understand the power behind this idea, you can start using 14 of the most powerful words to attract money—*fast*—by tapping into the law of attraction and the natural power of energy. I'm telling you, I *truly* believe that these 14 words are some of the most powerful ones you can ever say if you're looking to bring money into your life.

"So, now that you *really* understand that everything is just energy—even your words—the most important part is making this mantra actually work for you. If you want to start attracting more money into your life, you've got to *believe* in these words, wholeheartedly. It's super dangerous to just say them without *truly* believing in them, because then they won't have the impact you're looking for. But when you *do* believe, when you really feel it deep down, that's when the *amazing* things start happening."

———

FIRST THINGS FIRST: you have to agree with me that you're ready to let go of the statement "I don't know how." I don't know how the money will come. I don't know how this will work out. I don't know how... That's what I used to think, but once I replaced those subconscious belief systems with positive money beliefs, I realized I didn't need to know how.

Instead of telling you in theory, let me share a crazy story from my own life. I was 20 years old, doing success and money affirmations and practicing the law of attraction. I had dropped out of college, backpacked around the world, and wrote a book about it. All the publishing companies said no, so I had to self-publish. They told me I had to sell 10,000 copies for them to take me seriously. Well, I ended up selling 40,000 copies of that book, got a book deal with Penguin Random House and many other publishers, and my life changed financially. It all happened because I let go of "how." I didn't know how I would sell 40,000 copies; I just started. As Bob Marley used to say, "If you don't start somewhere, you're never going to get nowhere."

The next key to making these 14 words work for you is knowing what you want and where you're going. What you want is your goal—what do you really want financially? Most people never truly decide because they keep saying, "I don't know how." So, they don't even set their sails; they don't make a clear decision about what they want because they don't think they can get it. Don't let your fear of "how" stop you from defining what you want.

Now, before I give you these 14 words, here's something that I used to think sounded like total nonsense. Ten years ago, if the roles were reversed and you were telling me this, I wouldn't have believed it. But most of the reasons you block money in your life stem from childhood trauma, memories, and associations. "I don't know how" is often code for deeper childhood trauma or negative belief systems about your own inferiority.

So, you've got to uncover what's behind that "I don't know how." What are the deeper memories, the deeper triggers, the childhood emotions, traumas, and beliefs? Danielle Bernock famously said, "Trauma is personal. It does not disappear if it's not validated. When it's ignored or invalidated, the silent screams continue internally, heard only by the one held captive. When someone enters the pain and hears the screams, healing can begin.

But here's the thing: those old traumas, negative emotions, and beliefs don't just magically disappear. They have a way of re-manifesting and resurfacing in our lives, over and over, until we finally take the steps to clear them. And for a lot of people, that includes deep-rooted financial trauma.

The number one cause for divorce is financial issues. If you heard your parents arguing about not having enough money, if your dad guilted your mom for being the one always making it, or if your parents grew up in a bad economic time or had a poor financial upbringing, all of these ideas stick with you. People who hate money, who hate rich people, or think they're not good enough, smart enough, or that they need to go to an Ivy League school or even college at all—it's just a laundry list that never ends. But you can clear it now.

As I give you these 14 words, think about these questions: Do you think you're not good enough? Do you think you're too young or too old? Is it too late for you? Did your parents talk badly to you or about you, saying you're not smart enough, you're not deserving, or you're stupid? Maybe you have a traumatic memory, like reading in class in third grade, and you messed up some words. Then, some kid started laughing at you, and everyone else joined in, making you feel stupid. Since then, you've always associated being stupid with speaking in public. But now, you need to be a better speaker to make more money.

Whatever it is, what's the deep childhood trauma or negative memory about money that you can recall? Take a moment to really think about it—maybe it's a memory of your parents arguing about money, or a belief you've held onto for years that you're not good enough to earn what you desire. Just take a deep breath, and with full intention, say, "I'm ready to let it go."

As you bring this belief to the surface, you're not going to let it hold you back any longer. Instead, you're going to replace it with this powerful 14-word affirmation about money. This shift will make money flow like crazy into your life, opening up new opportunities in both expected and unexpected ways.

Take a deep breath and repeat these words with me: **"Money flows like crazy to me in expected and unexpected ways. I am financially blessed."** You can also add, "I'm so happy and grateful" at the beginning: **"I'm so happy and grateful money flows to me like crazy."**

Now, it doesn't maybe come to you. You don't hope that it will come. It's not a "maybe one day" kind of thing. It's not, "Oh man, I have so many issues; will I be able to do it?" It's none of that anymore. Money flows to you. Money flows like crazy in expected and unexpected ways.

Wayne Dyer used to say, "I'm realistic, I expect miracles." Expect miracles. Miracles are normal. Money comes to you in expected and unexpected ways. Say it, feel it. If you had to imagine or pretend that you were financially blessed or excited about financial opportunities in your life, how would that feel? Something really good just happened—you got that phone call, that email, whatever it is. Something really good financially has just happened. How does it feel? Feels good, right? Maybe it makes you smile a little. Maybe you say, "Isn't it wonderful? Isn't it wonderful?"

This shift, however cheesy or corny it may sound, moves your energy into alignment with money. When you move your energy or consciousness into the frequency of prosperity and abundance instead of lack and limitation, your reality changes. It's the same way that when you tune to a country station, you get country music—you don't get rap or rock. You get country because you've tuned into that frequency of sound. Now, you're tuning into the frequency of your own consciousness.

Repeat these 14 words again: **"Money flows to me like crazy in expected and unexpected ways. I am financially blessed."**

To truly get the best results from this practice, I highly recommend you take a little time each day to write these affirmations down. Make it a habit, a daily ritual, for at least the next 14 days. Fourteen powerful words for 14 consecutive days. The key is consistency. Write it down once a day, without skipping, and choose a method that feels right for you. You can jot it down on an index card you carry with you, write it in your journal, scribble it on a whiteboard you see daily, or even get creative and use lipstick on your bathroom mirror. The more places you see it, the better it will sink into your subconscious.

"Money flows to me like crazy in expected and unexpected ways. I am financially blessed."

By consistently putting these words in front of you, you're reinforcing the energy of abundance and sending a clear message to the universe. It's about repetition and belief, so make sure you're fully present as you write. This small, simple practice can start to shift your mindset, allowing you to feel more aligned with the flow of money and the blessings that are on their way to you.

Lets Play Eye Spy

———

Declutter You Surroundings

Once you remove certain items from your home or bedroom that are subconsciously blocking money, according to the ancient practice of feng shui, money will start chasing you. You may not even realize that all over your house there are these little subconscious associations—basically subliminal messages—that are blocking money from coming into your life. I'm going to show you exactly what you

might need to remove to help the money start flowing.

One key step is removing clutter to restore the flow of energy. We often feel constricted when things are too cluttered, which is why getting rid of what we don't need and tidying up is so powerful. There's that famous book, *The Magic of Tidying Up*, which explains how clutter blocks the flow of energy—or chi, or life force. It prevents new opportunities from entering your life by creating a state of subconscious stress or stagnation. This clutter can tie you to the past and block your financial progress. The mess around us is a reflection of blocks in our financial life. So, focus on removing unnecessary items from your bedroom, particularly anything that's in plain sight.

The reason this is so important is that even if we become used to it, we don't really notice it anymore—it's not that it's good; it's that we've become desensitized to it. However, our subconscious is still picking up on all this stress and constriction, which is blocking the flow of money. You can donate items you no longer use. If some things just need to be thrown away, don't hold on to them. Many people keep things they don't even want or use, but they're afraid to let go. I invite you to take a look at where you can free up space.

There's a story in one of the books I read about someone having financial problems. I think it was a book by Dr. Joseph Murphy. A person came to him for financial help because they needed to sell their house, not because they wanted to, but because they desperately needed the money. He told them to get the house in the shape that someone would want to buy. He said something interesting would happen when they did that. So, they cleaned up the house, fixed the blinds, and got everything dialed in. Before they even put the house on the market, they realized they loved their home more than they thought, and they felt a sense of wealth, abundance, and gratitude. Shortly after that, they got the financial breakthrough they needed without having to sell the house.

A lot of the things you want are closer than they appear—like the message in the side mirrors of our cars. It's just that there are little subconscious blocks holding you back.

Number two is to remove broken items to eliminate scarcity or fear energy. What I invite you to do is get rid of any broken or damaged things you've held onto because they symbolize lack. They represent a fear that more abundance may not come to you. Subliminally, this is programming you to stay in the same financial position. In feng shui, broken items reinforce the idea that you're okay with less, or that you can just make do without abundance. It's like saying, "Just be happy with what you have," which is great, but we're also meant for more. If we don't embrace that second part, we can get stuck rationalizing why it's okay to be broke, which isn't what the universe intended for us.

This might look like holding onto broken electronics, a leaky faucet, or a chair you've duct-taped together to keep using. It could be something like a pair of shoes with a massive hole, where you could buy new shoes but you're afraid money might not come. You're stuck with a hole in your shoe, your toe sticking out, and that's a symbol of fear. For everyone, it's something different. I think we all know what those things are, and I invite you to take a look at that and feel into it. You are worthy, and there is more to come. If you let go of the fear, as

Kyle Cease says, "You can't see what's coming if you're still holding onto what's left." Take a deep breath and say to yourself, "I am deserving of success. I am deserving of success." It may seem silly, like "this is silly" but there's a difference between consciously agreeing and actually reprogramming your subconscious. Subconsciously, you might not believe you're good enough for more. One way to uninstall that virus from your operating system is to look around and see what you're holding onto, not out of love but out of fear and scarcity. That fear and scarcity are reinforced every day in the comfort of your own home.

Number three is to remove unpaid bills or even bills you've already paid but have kept lying around, whether in your living room, bedroom, or another space where we tend to put stuff like that. We all have that place where we store financial paperwork, like unpaid bills, which carry all this energy and stress. Maybe we keep them out on the counter because we're planning to pay them in 30 or 60 days, but don't have the money to deal with them now. Or perhaps the amount is too much, and we just don't want to face it at the moment.

But what happens is, we leave these papers in a spot where we subconsciously see them every day, even if we're not consciously paying attention. In feng shui, your home is meant to be a place of rest. Having these constant reminders of financial stress visible keeps us trapped in an energy that ties us to more money problems. The energy of these documents or bills—like maybe it's a ticket you're unable to pay—carries stress with it. When you go to sleep, your subconscious mind is in overdrive, and it starts to anchor or cement whatever dominant subliminal energy you've been seeing or feeling during the day.

That's why I always recommend using success hypnosis at night. It's one of the fastest ways to reprogram your subconscious mind to bring more money into your life. Essentially, just before sleep, your conscious mind shuts off, giving you direct access to reprogram your subconscious mind. You are meant for financial abundance, and once you really grasp that, that's when all the good things start to come.

Number four is a really big one that I didn't even think about until recently, and it's about removing negative artwork. You might not even realize it's negative because it could be expensive, look cool, or seem nice. As you pass by it in your home, you don't really notice, but what I invite you to do is sit and look at it for a minute—not just glance at the colors or the style, but really feel the frequency of it.

I had a personal experience with this a few years ago when we were renting a beautiful home with an ocean view from the master bedroom. It was a furnished home, with a lot of expensive items. One night, I couldn't sleep, and I turned the lights on dimly. I sat up in bed and looked around, and there was this one painting that I passed by all the time—it was right in the middle of the bedroom. I must have walked by it dozens of times a day and never noticed anything, but when I really looked at it, I got bad vibes. It gave me a feeling of sadness, fear, or insecurity. The painting itself was beautifully done, but it showed a person looking away with their shoulders hunched, and it carried this energy of fear, like there was a lot to be afraid of in the world. Maybe that's what the artist intended, but subconsciously, I had been picking up that energy all day long without realizing it.

It might be paintings, pictures, objects, or other pieces of art in your home. You may not have even put them there, but go through and take a closer look. If something gives off the opposite energy of abundance or confidence, it's time to remove it. There are many studies on subliminal messaging and how it can control our behavior, future decisions, and ultimately our lives. So, it's important to remove anything that's putting out negative energy.

This is why I always say, "Brainwash yourself before the world brainwashes you." It sounds like a strange phrase, but we're all brainwashed in some way. Your personality and belief systems are forms of brainwashing, whether it's positive, negative, helpful, or harmful. We're brainwashed by the world and our environment every day, so you don't want your home to carry that energy. By removing negative imprints in your space, you can reprogram your subconscious for financial abundance instead.

Now, the next step is to go on a scavenger hunt in your own home and see which of these negative imprints speak to you. Just like playing "I Spy" with my daughter in the car, where we look for specific things to pass the time, you can play a game where you look for things in your home that carry that negative energy. Clear them out to make way for abundance and wealth to flow into your life. This simple shift can change everything. You might already be working hard, but if you're not seeing results, it could be due to subconscious blocks that are holding you back. Removing them is one of the quickest and fastest ways to free yourself up for success.

The Law Of Assumption

———

Unlock The Invisible And Manifest Your Desires By Living As If
They're Already Yours

A fter you do this, everything you visualize will come true quicker
and faster than you ever thought possible.

Here's the thing: you can't escape the Law of Assumption. You can use it to get exactly what you want in life, or it can use you, drawing in everything you fear and don't want. Our understanding of the world is largely shaped by our five senses: sight, hearing, taste, smell, and touch. though humans can not see feel or understand the vast spectrum of energies the universe holds using the senses we have evolved in the short time we have been on this world. When we rely solely on these senses to define reality, we overlook a significant part of the universe that remains invisible.

Take the electromagnetic spectrum, for example: it spans a huge range of wavelengths and frequencies of light that we cannot detect. Humans can only see a small portion of visible light. Beyond this visible light, there's ultraviolet, which we can't see, and infrared, which we can sometimes feel but cannot visually detect. Our visual limitations mean we miss a full picture of what's happening around us. The same applies to our hearing—humans can only detect frequencies from about 200 to 20,000 hertz, leaving out many other frequencies. I remember my mom using a dog whistle when I was young; I couldn't hear it, but the dogs could. Our sense of smell and other senses are similarly limited. There's so much energy we can't detect, and everything you want is just energy, too.

Think about it: the house, car, money, job, relationships, health, future, and life you desire are all forms of energy. We only perceive a small portion of this energy, so when we rely on our five senses to determine what's possible, we limit ourselves. It's not even a full representation of reality because it's such a narrow band of energy. Remember, "lack of evidence is not evidence of lack." What we perceive as solid matter is made up of particles and waves of energy constantly in motion, much of which we can't see or sense. If we create our future based only on what we can perceive with our five senses, we'll only be able to create more of the same, keeping us in a limited cycle.

You are an infinite being, and everything you want already exists as a possibility in the quantum field. The subatomic particles are simply energy waves, often outside the visible spectrum, but you can bring them into reality. I'm going to show you how to do it. This is important because most people create their future based on their past experiences. Yet, everything around you- the phone or book you're reading it on—is an example of someone being a visionary and creating something that couldn't initially be seen. Every tangible thing in reality first existed in someone's imagination. To manifest your desires, you have to move beyond the physical and focus on the invisible.

This shift allows you to start bending time, enabling you to create what you want quicker and faster. This is where most people encounter the Law of Attraction. However, most Law of Attraction teachings come from a third-dimensional perspective. They suggest that if you don't see what you want in the world around you, you need to change it. But that's still operating from the evidence of your five senses, and this is where Neville Goddard's teachings on the Law of Assumption become so important. I'm going to show you how to use the Law of Assumption to go from wanting things to actually having what you want. It's pretty simple—especially for children, who haven't yet been deeply programmed to believe in the limitations of what they can see and touch.

Most people struggle to leverage the Law of Assumption because it requires a major shift in belief—to trust in what you cannot see and to assume a reality that's only visible with your eyes closed. Today, people are incorrectly taught to manifest by visualizing their desires temporarily. This is how the Law of Attraction is often taught. The issue here is that after you visualize what you want, your mind has a habit of reverting its focus to your present reality—what you perceive with your five senses. This re-focus creates a serious limitation because if your attention shifts back to your current reality after visualizing, you will simply create more of the same reality.

It's like setting a new GPS destination but continuing to follow the old directions. Without understanding the Law of Assumption, you get stuck in a feedback loop of repeated, unmanifested desires—a cycle where nothing changes because the majority of your mental energy remains locked in your current reality and senses.

Now, this concept might make sense in theory, but you might wonder, "Where's the proof that this approach actually works better?" Well, before I explain the three steps, let me share that when I first learned these principles, I made $8,525 in a year (that's the exact number on my tax return). Within 24 months, I had a million-dollar business. So, yes, I can say with 100% certainty that this works.

The first step is to stop thinking about what you don't want or what you currently have. We talked about how we're programmed to focus on what we lack, even though we know what we desire. We want more money, but identify with being broke. We want to fall in love, but identify with being single or heartbroken, thinking there are "no good partners" out there. Every desire has two elements: the presence of what you want or the absence of it. If we haven't trained ourselves to disregard the evidence of our five senses, then even if we set goals, we're still primarily thinking from a place of lack.

Neville Goddard spoke extensively about the illusion of life—how our assumptions manifest so convincingly that we attribute unwanted experiences to "bad luck." But in reality, we subconsciously put attention on what we don't want, recreating the feedback loop and experiencing the same old reality. This is also why, when we're caught in a cycle of negative thoughts, life seems to get progressively worse, providing more evidence for these thoughts.

In response, people are often told to "visualize more," but when our minds have been conditioned our whole lives to live within the limits of our senses, that extra effort doesn't lead anywhere new. The real answer is disentangling our minds from our current reality.

The first step is to write a detailed journal entry about the future you've envisioned, exactly as if you're journaling about your day today. Date it 12 months from now and write in the present tense, detailing what your life is like with your wishes fulfilled. Describe in detail how excited and grateful you feel, as if you're already experiencing it.

The second step is to read this journal entry aloud, first thing in the morning and three times before bed. The third step is to mentally rehearse this journal entry with your mind and eyes closed as you fall asleep. Neville says that all creation takes place in the state of sleep, or in a state similar to sleep—the drowsy, sleepy state. The science behind this is clear: as you fall asleep, your brain waves slow into theta, a meditative brainwave state. In theta, your brain's electromagnetic waves take you out of rational thinking and ordinary consciousness, dissociating you from your five senses and the current space-time reality.

This is why visualization doesn't work for most people in a fully alert state. When you're in a normal, wakeful brainwave state, your mind gets stuck in logic, refuting new ideas and affirmations. However, your imagination is a preview of life's coming attractions. As you fall asleep, focus on feeling the details of your journal entry. Imagine what it feels like to walk into your dream house, increase your income, or receive a promotion. Picture the smile on your face and the excitement you feel.

Feel the emotions tied to attracting unexpected clients or taking a walk on the beach with a new love.

I use success hypnosis. I've been doing this for ten years, and for quite a few years, I even played it all night. The reason I do this is because when your brain is in these slower wave states, you are able to gain direct access to your subconscious mind. Many people don't realize that's why visualization and other manifestation techniques don't work for them—they're doing it all in the daytime, in a heightened brainwave state, where the logical mind intervenes, projecting the old patterns even if you're unaware of it.

My routine includes turning on success hypnosis, reading my journal entries out loud, closing my eyes, and immersing myself in the experience. Recently, we moved into a dream house my wife has wanted for years. I would imagine opening the door, seeing the mountains over the pool in the backyard, and every time my mind wandered, the hypnosis would bring me back. This is why you can begin to see changes quickly—when you fall asleep, you disconnect from the physical world, making it easier to reprogram your subconscious mind to attract what you want.

Harnessing Quantum Energy

Transform Thoughts into Financial Abundance

There are a million videos out there promising the most powerful manifestation technique and a million motivational books you can choose from. It gets boring. You start to wonder what's real, what isn't, who's just reciting something, and who has actually had real results. In this technique, I'm going to give you a quantum money method that I used to manifest my dream house and dream car, all within a couple of months. I'll share the proof and exactly how I used this technique to bring more money into my life, and how you can do

it quicker and easier than you ever thought possible.

Now, step number one is to focus on quantum money. In quantum physics, the Observer Effect refers to the idea that the act of observing a particle influences its behavior. In certain experiments, a particle's path isn't determined until it's observed, suggesting that observing with your mind directly influences reality.

So let's bring this idea to money. We often think of money as paper bills, coins, or digits in a bank account, but at its core, money is a form of energy—a medium of exchange used to facilitate transactions. So how does this relate to quantum physics and the Observer Effect? Imagine money as a flowing stream of energy, like water in a river. Your thoughts, beliefs, and feelings about money are like rocks in this river, either obstructing the flow of money or helping you direct it where you want it to go.

In quantum terms, your observations or thoughts about money—whether it's "I never have enough money," "I'm not smart enough," or "I always attract wealth"—influence your financial reality. They either place rocks in the river or move them away. Just like in quantum physics, where your observation affects reality, if you're constantly observing a lack of money, focusing on debt, or stressing about bills, this negative focus can manifest as continued financial struggle. You're placing rocks that obstruct the flow of the money river. But if you shift your focus and start observing positively, like practicing gratitude for what you have or feeling grateful for things yet to come, you visualize a future of abundance and feel it deeply. You're effectively changing the path of money in your life, rearranging the rocks to create a smooth flow of the money river.

This leads us to Big Idea number two: transmuting energy into money. I'm going to give you a powerful technique that can help you unlock what feels like god-like powers, allowing you to influence and change reality through your mind—especially when it comes to money. But first, let's dive a bit deeper into the science so this technique works even faster for you.

In science, there are some powerful laws, like the Law of Perpetual Transmutation of Energy, which states that energy is always in motion and can change form, but it never disappears. This law says that everything in the universe—including thoughts, emotions, and all physical objects—are forms of energy that are constantly vibrating or changing states. To simplify, imagine attracting or repelling money as energy, like water. Water can be liquid, solid, gas, or steam, but it's still water; it just changes form depending on the conditions around it.

Now, think of your thoughts and feelings about money as that same kind of energy. Just like water, positive thoughts and feelings about money act like warmth that can melt ice into a flowing river. When you think positively about money, saying things like, "I am capable of earning money" or "Money flows to me easily," you're like a warm sunny day melting the ice, allowing this river of money to flow and then negative thoughts and feelings about money are like cold air that can freeze the flowing energy of money, blocking it, just like saying "I'll never have enough" or "I'm always struggling financially." It's like being a cold winter day, causing the flow of money to slow down or even stop. But since energy is omnipresent and perpetually transforming, the quantum reality of the money you desire is that it's already there—it's just waiting for you to call it into your life.

This leads us to Big Idea number three: how to become a generator of wealth energy so you can bring it into your life. To illustrate, something amazing happened recently. My family and I just bought our dream house. It's the first home we've ever had that truly feels like we want to be there forever. While on vacation, we finalized the purchase, and once we moved in, I hadn't spent much time in my old office. My three-year-old daughter loves to come into my office, where I have a big picture of my mentor, Bob Proctor. She often comes in and talks to the picture, saying things like, "Where's Bob? Oh, hi, Bob!" I also have a huge chalkboard in my office where she likes to draw.

One day, she noticed my vision board on the side of the chalkboard. She looked at it and said, "Oh, Daddy, look—it's our house, our new house." I realized I hadn't even thought about my vision board recently, but there on the board was an image very similar to our new house: a living room with glass walls that opens up to a pool with a beautiful view, just like ours with the mountains in the background. She looked around and said, "That looks like your new black car," pointing to the top of the board where I had also put an image of my dream car—a matte black convertible AMG E53 Mercedes. I had completely forgotten about placing these exact images on my vision board.

That's the power of this technique, and it's very simple. Start by printing out images of things you want from Google Images. It could be a house in the mountains, a specific color car, a family on the beach for more vacations, or even an image representing the ideal body you envision for yourself. Whatever it is, print it out and place it on your vision board.

DO THIS TO MANIFEST EVERYTHING

Once you've done that, here's a simple process to follow. What I do is play my affirmations success hypnosis that I had my narrator narrate on audible softly in the background, activating different parts of my brain through auditory functions. While listening, I look at each image on my vision board, one by one, using my senses to visualize. For example, I'll focus on the car I want, close my eyes for a moment, and practice visualizing it clearly, just like you would with your hand. If you stare at your hand long enough and then close your eyes, you'll still see it clearly, right?

Move through each image on your board, practicing visualizing each item as reality. Don't move to the next image until you evoke a positive feeling, which is a key sign that the technique is working. As you go through, repeat "Thank you, thank you, thank you, God" or "Thank you, thank you, thank you" for each item. This helps your brain believe that you not only can have these things but already do. It signals your brain to begin rearranging reality from a subatomic level to bring these desired things into your life.

This technique has worked wonders for me, and everything you want already exists—you just have to bring it into being. I'd love to hear your results using this technique and share your success story in a future book. Comment on the review page with your story, and let me know where you're tuning in from! I'm in the beautiful Southwest United States and would love to know your city, state, country, or even planet! Also, don't forget I have affirmations hipnosis audiobooks out now on Audible which I use daily so if youd care to join me listening to them you can find them by searching Archer Sterling Affirmations on Audible.

Isnt It Wonderful?

———

Try This For 21 Days To Attract Amazing Things

I'm going to give you a very simple technique where all you need to do is press the middle of your forehead for 60 seconds, and you can use this as a key to create whatever you want in life. This chapter is a blend of EFT tapping and acupressure. We all know that acupuncture has been around for thousands of years as an ancient Chinese medicine practice based on 14 energy meridians or centers in the body. With acupuncture, they use a needle, but with acupressure, you use your finger to tap into blocked energy. Here, we'll be combining both acupressure and tapping.

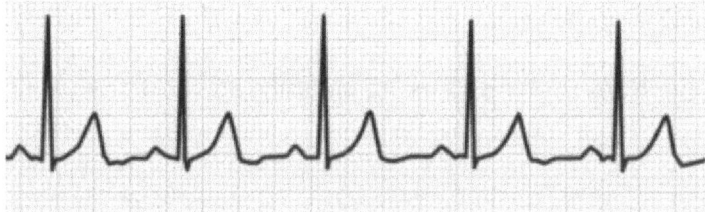

First, it's important to know that all you are is energy. These images should look familiar, right? EKGs and ECGs measure electrical brain and heart activity. Essentially, we're all just fields of energy. Due to old emotions, trauma, and negative thinking, this energy can get blocked, stopping you from attracting what you want in life.

This simple technique will break down into a few easy steps and, once you learn it, will only take about 60 seconds. It will specifically help you open your third eye, become better at visualizing, and start attracting what you want more quickly and easily.

Step 1: Start with one of my favorite quotes from Bob Proctor: *"If you can see it in your mind, you can hold it in your hand."* Build such a clear picture that even a stranger would know what you want. For example, when I started visualizing, I pictured my book blowing up. I would imagine refreshing the browser in my mind and seeing my book go viral, then jumping up to tell my wife, "My book went viral!" Create a clear picture of exactly what you want—whether it's walking on the beach with your soulmate, moving into a new house, shaking hands with clients, seeing a big bank balance, or finishing an album or book.

Step 2: Use your index or middle finger to rhythmically tap the point between your eyebrows, also known as your third eye or pineal gland. This is the focal point for manifesting here in the 3D, physical dimension. Close your eyes and tap about 20 times, rhythmically, as you breathe in and out. Relax your eyebrows and facial muscles. As you relax and breathe, you may notice lights in colors like white, blue, or yellow. Just observe the light.

This warm-up helps engage your energy, shifting attention from your physical body to your energy.

Step 3: After you've tapped and relaxed, stop tapping and gently press that spot, engaging the acupressure technique. As you lightly press, you'll really start to see the light and energy. Transfer this energy into your clear mental picture. Since energy isn't created or destroyed—only transferred—this serves as a Kickstarter to help clarify your vision. Breathe deeply as you focus on the picture of what you want: selling a house or car, seeing yourself with the money, or being with your soulmate. Hold that picture as you breathe.

Step 4: Once you clearly see the picture in your third eye, repeat the simple words, *"Isn't it wonderful?"* several times. This affirms to your brain that it's already wonderful, reinforcing that what you desire is already happening.

This is the auto-suggestion—using a hypnotic suggestion. Instead of seeing the picture and wondering, *How do I make it a reality?*, you're affirming, just like Neville Goddard says, *"Isn't it wonderful?"*

Once you finish, bring your hands together and rub them together then separate them just slightly. When you do, you start to feel the energy a bit. It reminds you of the EKG chart of your heart rate, of yourself as an energy field, just breathing in and out, feeling that energy. This reminds you that energy is never created or destroyed; it's only transferred into different states. When you realize that, the picture you want is already real and coming to you.

This is a simple 60-second technique. Whether you're in the office, in the bathroom, waking up in the morning, or having a negative thought, all you do is stop and call upon that picture—see your YouTube channel going viral, making sales, being with your soulmate, feeling happy, or living in your dream house. Once you have the picture, tap, breathe rhythmically, and notice the white or blue lights. Then, press gently under that light, bringing all your attention to focus on it and transferring that energy into the picture. Now you see your dream as a reality.

Once you see it, affirm: *"Isn't it wonderful?"* When you feel the energy shift and the excitement, keep affirming, *"Isn't it wonderful?"* It's on the way. This exercise, only 60 seconds, can be used daily.

Here are a few quick points to know. In 2015, UCLA's neuroscience division conducted an interesting study that showed how self-affirmation builds new neural pathways when repeated. Nobel Prize-winning scientist Eric Kandel also demonstrated that when you learn something new or perform a new activity, you double the neural connections in your brain. But within three weeks, if the new activity isn't repeated, those connections are cut by 50%. Both UCLA and Nobel Prize-winning research show us that repetition is how you change your brain, your life, and your certainty.

I encourage you to do this every day for 21 days. Read this chapter through once to get the hang of it. Remember: see the picture, tap until you see the colors, relax your brows, breathe deeply, move to acupressure, and transfer the blue or white energy into the picture, ending with *"Isn't it wonderful?"*

To make this even more powerful, engage your senses to reach the subconscious. I have a multiple affirmation hipnosis audiobooks on audible . I created it for myself, and now, thousands of people have downloaded and used it all over the world. If you play it softly while doing this exercise, you'll engage your brain more deeply, build new neural pathways, and start hardwiring that picture into your brain.

Here's the amazing part: once it's hardwired, your brain becomes a reward-seeking mechanism, making it show up in expected and unexpected ways.

Have you ever wondered why some people seem to turn their lives around, becoming really successful and manifesting everything they want? In this chapter, I'll explain exactly how I went from zero dollars as a college dropout to attracting over five million dollars in less than a few years when I was just in my mid-20s. This is due to something called the mirror principle. Maybe you've heard of it, maybe you haven't, or maybe you've seen a video where someone talks about it online. The idea is simple: your outside world is a mirror that reflects what's going on inside of you. Your friends, family, school, and how much money you make are all connected through your thoughts, feelings, and beliefs. What's happening inside your heart and mind is what controls your world, and I'm going to explain exactly how you can use this to quickly change your life.

First, I'll start with my story. I'm actually in my backyard right now at sunrise. It all began when I was 22 years old, and things were not going very well. My girlfriend, Ashley—who is now my wife—was about $10,000 in credit card debt. She was in that debt because I wasn't making enough money to cover basic necessities, and my business that year had only made about $8,500. I was trying to fix everything around me with productivity hacks and other tactics, but none of it was actually working. Then, I realized that the shift had to start from within, and once I made that shift, things changed quickly. Within the first 24 months, I made a million dollars, and everything just kept building and building. This transformation was all because of the mirror principle.

So why does your inner world affect your outer world? Everything is made up of energy, even though it may not look like it. Scientists have shown that 99% of all physical matter is just energy. The mirror principle is based on an ancient concept called the Law of Correspondence, which means "as above, so below; as within, so without." You've probably heard that before, and all it means is that your physical world is a reflection of your inner world.

There are three levels of existence in using the mirror principle. There's the physical realm, which we can see, smell, taste, and touch—it's our homes, bodies, bank accounts, the tangible world around us. Then there's the mental realm, which is our thoughts, beliefs, and ideas. Lastly, we have the spiritual realm, the world of energy, vibration, and feelings. We can't see it, but we can feel it. Everything in the physical world is just energy, but it's our thoughts and feelings that control how our reality shapes itself.

This is where the magic really happens. The pictures in your mind create emotions, and those emotions ultimately control your outside world. But what often happens is that we get caught up in our environment: we look at the mirror of life and say, *I am broke.* This thought then affects our feelings; we start feeling stressed about money, or maybe we feel lonely or sad because we don't have a partner. The outside world begins to control our thinking and feeling, which locks us into creating the same experiences over and over.

What I invite you to do is to let go of your five senses and start focusing on the feelings of what it is that you want to create. I like to turn this into a fun game, so I invite you to play this game with me: Imagine you knew your future partner was going to walk into your life tomorrow at 11 a.m. You don't know them yet, but you know they're coming. How would you feel? Or how would you feel if you knew that next week, there would be five hundred thousand dollars in your bank account, and all your debts would be gone? If you knew you were going to get a raise, how would you feel?

Now, I'm not saying those things will happen by tomorrow at 11 a.m., but consider the feeling you'd have if they were possible. Controlling your feelings from your inner world, rather than allowing your feelings to be controlled by the outer world, is exactly how you change your outer world.

Once your feelings no longer match the level of your environment—like Bob Proctor used to say, *"Does your thinking control your bank account, or does your bank account control your thinking?"* My bank account controlled my thinking because I didn't have much money, maybe around $8,500. In that mindset, I couldn't create anything new. It's like looking in the mirror, seeing a piece of spinach stuck in your teeth, and trying to use white-out to change the mirror. It's impossible! You have to change the thing creating the reflection—your teeth, in this case, and the spinach on them. Similarly, you need to change your inner world to shift what it reflects.

So what I did was very simple. I created a hypnosis audiobooks for myself. Every day, I listened to this one hypnosis to start reprogramming my subconscious mind to think and feel as if I already had what I wanted. I wanted to get a book published and be successful, but none of that was happening. When I looked at my outside world, I would think, *This sucks. It's not working.* So, I shut off my five senses, listened to a hypnosis, and practiced thinking and feeling as if I already had hundreds of thousands of readers and was a published author making millions. I practiced feeling this reality while the success hypnosis reprogrammed my subconscious mind.

What you're doing with this is changing your inner world, which shifts your outer world. This is how you master the mirror principle: by taking control of your subconscious mind.

My life really changed when I removed one money block I didn't even know I had. Bob Proctor told me, *"Here's your biggest money block. Once you remove this, money's going to start coming to you from everywhere."* I wasn't entirely sure if I believed him, but I removed that block, and suddenly, money began flowing in from all directions in amounts beyond anything I could have imagined. I'm going to show you how to do it too.

One of the first things I learned from Bob was that I wasn't comfortable with money at all. I wanted money—not because I was materialistic, but because I wanted freedom. I wanted to do what I wanted without checking prices. I wanted to buy what I wanted at the grocery store without making decisions based on the cost. I wanted true freedom. At the same time, I thought I was "spiritual," and somehow, that made me see money as a negative thing. So, I wasn't attracting it. Bob helped me realize that how much money you earn is directly tied to how you think and feel about this one statement: *It's my right to be rich.*

Now, what do you feel when you say that? Say it to yourself: *It's my right to be rich.* Or *God wants me to be rich.* How does that feel? For me, it felt weird. It felt uncomfortable, even untrue. My beliefs wanted to argue with those statements, but I didn't fully realize it because it was all happening subconsciously.

Once Bob pointed that out to me, I realized that was my biggest problem. It wasn't that I wasn't working hard enough—I was. It wasn't that I needed to start a business—I already had one. The problem was that I didn't believe it was my right to be rich, or that God wanted me to be rich. I thought money wasn't "spiritual" or "holy." I thought that money was made by "bad" people and that I just needed enough to survive.

Now, think about it: imagine if you talked about someone else like that—like your boyfriend, girlfriend, or spouse. Saying things like, *"You're unnecorcory evil, but I'll be happy without you."* How long would they stick around? Not long! They might just walk out without even saying goodbye. You're in the kitchen chopping up dinner, talking about how much they're "the root of all evil," and you turn around, and they're gone. No one would stay!

Right? Just like they say, but we do this with money too. And money "has ears and hears when you call" That's why I'm so big on hypnosis, because we don't even realize all these negative beliefs we carry around about money. One of the things I'm most grateful for in my life is learning this from Bob Proctor, and even just thinking about that makes me emotional. The guy changed my life by helping me see that the only reason I wasn't getting what I wanted was my own perception and thinking. It wasn't the world, my bank account, my business, customers, clients, the economy, my parents, my teachers, or any old business partner who let me down. None of that. The problem was me—my mind, my energy, and my beliefs. Once I accepted that it was my right to be rich, things changed.

So, say it with me: *"It's my right to be rich."* This is why it's so important to use hypnosis. You can get my affirmations hypnosis at Audible. It's all about reprogramming yourself for prosperity. How can you expect money to come to you if you're still thinking and feeling like a broke person? That's exactly what Bob helped me realize.

If you believe in a creator or universal intelligence, don't you think it would want you to have what you desire? Alan Watts said it best: *"You can't get wet by the word water."* So, whatever you call this force—whether it's God, spirit, or cosmic intelligence—don't you think it wants you to experience all of life's abundance? God gave people the ideas for inventions, homes, businesses, and everything in creation. Your desire for more money or abundance is really a desire to experience more of what God created, and that's a powerful way to look at life.

Now there's no resistance—you've dropped any money blocks or feelings of unworthiness. It's not about whether you're "good enough"; it's simply that God wants you to have it. God wants you to thrive, to have that successful business, to buy that car, pay off your mortgage, own your dream home, and retire your parents. If God wants it for you, and what you want also wants you, then any thoughts of limitation or unworthiness are just illusions.

It's amazing, isn't it? Just reflecting on this has shifted my energy and made me feel even more open to achieving my goals. So, I invite you to comment down below: *"God wants me to be rich,"* or *"It's my right to be rich."* When you truly believe that, things start happening fast: the right opportunities, that phone call, or that person who can help you all start showing up as soon as your perception shifts. It's exciting, because now you start to see just how much abundance you can create. And remember, it's not really "us" doing it—it's God working through us.

Milton Keynes UK
Ingram Content Group UK Ltd.
UKHW030851111124
451035UK00001B/143